Charles Miller

Anna May Doan

Eleanor Winsor

Jean Doan

OF ROXABOXEN

THE
LEGACY of ROXABOXEN

A COLLECTION OF VOICES

For Donna—

Alice McLerran

OTHER BOOKS BY ALICE MCLERRAN

The Mountain That Loved a Bird (*1985*)
Secrets (*1990*)
Roxaboxen (*1991*)
I Want to Go Home (*1992*)
Dreamsong (*1992*)
Hugs (*1993*)
Kisses (*1993*)
The Ghost Dance (*1996*)
The Year of the Ranch (*1996*)

THE
LEGACY of ROXABOXEN

A COLLECTION OF VOICES

ALICE MCLERRAN

"That is question now;
And then comes answer like an Absey book.
King John, i, 9
Shakespeare

Absey & Company
Spring, Texas

Acknowledgements:

Sheet music covers © Warner Bros. Publications. All rights reserved. Used by permission.

Cover and one interior illustration from ROXABOXEN by Alice McLerran. Illustrated by Barbara Cooney. Ill: Copyright © 1991 by Barbara Cooney. By permission of Lothrop, Lee & Shepard Books, a division of William Morrow & Company, Inc..

The *Yuma Examiner* is no longer a functioning newspaper.

The *Yuma Sun* for excerpts of articles. Permissions granted.

ISBN 1-888842-08-3

To my loving and beloved Aunt Jean--and to Charles and Helen, as dear to Jean now as in the days when she followed her sisters up that hill.
A.M.

Contents

Introduction

For all their more elegant bindings, few commercially-published books have lasted as long or well as has *The History of Roxaboxan,* a small book proudly self-published by Marian Doan. More than eighty years have passed since Marian stitched her book's spine with white, sewing thread—but her voice still rings fresh and vibrant from its pages.

When this project began, I was pleased that Marian's work would at last be available to the public but anticipated nothing more than a facsimile edition of her handwritten book. Quickly, however, the planned publication evolved into a poignant collection of essays and graphics. Such a setting for Marian's small literary jewel lets the reader appreciate the character of the young author, the background of the history she relates, and the impact her 1916 book has had—an impact not only upon other writers but upon the very place her history celebrates.

What a child creates can matter. I rejoiced in the chance not simply to tell but to show that! I am both Marian Doan's daughter and a writer. At first, I assumed the setting needed for our facsimile was something I could provide single-handedly. It soon proved natural that other voices should join in the telling of the story. The memoirs of Marian's sister Frances offered an intimate portrait of the young author. To clarify or amplify points in that portrait, and to elucidate otherwise obscure parts of Marian's own text, I found myself drawing extensively on the memoirs of Marian's mother, May Cargill Doan. Throughout, I have made use of illuminating recollections and help with historical matters provided by Marian's sister Jean Black and by others throughout the Doan clan.

Intertwined in the pages that follow are voices spanning three generations. Along with Marian, they tell the story of what happened back in the early days of Roxaboxen and bring the history of that special place forward into the present day.

I am especially grateful to my cousin Walter Turner for permission to use portions from his mother's memoirs of her Yuma childhood and to my cousins Robin and George Dillard for preparing and sharing the family edition of May Cargill Doan's story of her life. Many of the photos and

Jean, Frances, Anna May, and Marian in front of house in Yuma. Circa 1915.

other graphic materials reproduced here come from my own collections; others have been made available by family, friends, and other sources. Those to whom I am indebted for graphic materials and for details of family and Yuma history, include virtually every relative and Roxaboxenite listed in "A Guide to the Doan Clan." I hope all my favorite cousins will forgive me if I do not list them here by name; I offer each one my gratitude. The photos of the author and cast of the play *Roxaboxen* were taken by Diane Peterson (cousin Leslie's daughter) and her husband, Marshall. Charles and Helen generously shared their own childhood pictures, and Larry Davis provided precious early photos of his late wife, Eleanor. Diligent searches of the Web by my cousin Frances Giffin led me to resources I might never otherwise have found, including World War I buff Troy Buddenhage, William Oleson of the Maritime Museum at San Pedro, and Bill Allen at the nearby Ft. MacArthur Museum.

During my researches in Yuma, there were many who were generous with their time, knowledge, and resources. Outstandingly helpful were Lisa Kniffin at the Yuma County Library, John Vaughn at the *Yuma Sun*, Carol Brooks at the Yuma Historical Society, Fred Croxen of Arizona Western College, and Marilyn Young, Mayor of the City of Yuma. I'm grateful as well to Yvonne Peach, whose hospitality always helps make my visits to Yuma feel like coming home.

I hope this presentation of Marian Doan's history will be of interest not only to those for whom the name "Roxaboxen" already carries a hint of magic but also to teachers and parents who nurture the skills of young authors—and most of all, to those young authors themselves.

As I relate in the essay describing my discovery of the original book, another of Marian's sisters—Anna May Darrah—once recorded for her family a tape on which she reads aloud the text of her sister's book. After each chapter, Anna May adds details from her own memories of Roxaboxen. She ends the tape by saying, "Like its young historian, I guess I want Roxaboxen to live on forever."
So do I, Anna May.

Alice McLerran
Copenhagen, 1997

View from the balcony of the apartment where Alice wrote this introduction.

TWO

A Guide to the Doan Clan
And Certain Others Connected
With Roxaboxen

John Doan (1875-1935) and May Cargill Doan (1880-1967): parents of
the Doan girls

May Cargill
dressed for her sister's wedding
circa 1903

John Doan
An official photograph as
House Representative to the
State of Arizona
January 12, 1931-March 14, 1931
Special Session
December 28, 1931-January 9, 1932

The four Doan sisters:

Marian

Frances

Anna May

Jean

Marian (1905-1980)
        Married Herbert Enderton; two daughters, two sons
                Ann Pugh (1931)
                Alice McLerran (1933)
                Herbert Enderton (1936)
                Donald Enderton (1941)

Anna May (1907-1992)
        First marriage to Oliver White; two daughters
                Carol Drake (1935)
                Robin Dillard (1936)
    Second marriage to Nelson Darrah; two stepchildren
                Ruth Fleming (1936)
                Roger Darrah (1945)

Frances (1908-1996)
        Married Walter Turner; a son, a daughter
                Walter Turner Jr. (1931)
                Cynthia Turner (1936-1991)

Jean (1910)
        Married to William Black; a son, two daughters
                William Black (1939)
                Leslie Black (1941)
                Frances Black (1944)

Other notable Roxaboxenites:

Eleanor Winsor Davis
Marian's special friend.
(The girls' mothers were also close friends.)
The Winsor library was an important
resource of books to the young Doans.

Charles Miller
First knew the Doan family in Somerton,
later lived next door to them in Yuma.

Helen Dunbar Lucas
A friend especially dear to Jean.
Helen's mother was the elocution coach
for Marian's eighth-grade graduation
speech.

THREE

The Discovery

When my sister Ann and I were little, Mama always told us stories after she had tucked us into bed. Sometimes her stories would be traditional tales; more often they were ones invented just for us. But no tales were more laden with magic than the stories of a special town she and her sisters and their friends had created long ago on a desert hill in Yuma, Arizona — a hill called Roxaboxen. The mere name of the place always rang with magic for me.

I grew older. As I approached adolescence, I stopped calling my mother "Mama;" she became "Mother" for me instead. Little by little, the images of the stories she had once told us faded in my memory. Still, the sense of magic that surrounded Roxaboxen remained vivid, even if the details gradually became blurred.

Marian Doan with her first three children: Herbert in her arms, Ann in cape, Alice with box. Schofield Barracks, Hawaii, 1935. Two girls on left are unidentified.

Years after Mother's death, I wanted to attempt a picture-book text celebrating that special place and the power of imagination that created a community there. It seemed sad there was no way I could go back to Mama once more—no way to ask her to tell me all those stories again. Well, I reassured myself, her sisters would remember.

By that time—it must have been about 1986—all three of the surviving sisters lived in California, and I was in Illinois. My researches would have to begin by phone. I started with a call to my mother's youngest sister, Jean Black. "I'm trying to write a book about Roxaboxen," I explained. "Can you remember the details of what you all did there?"

"Oh, can I!" responded Jean. Gripping the receiver between shoulder and chin, I scrawled notes as rapidly as I could, trying to keep up with the flood of memories. But suddenly Jean broke off in mid-spate. "You know, your mother wrote a book about Roxaboxen," she said. "I'll send it to you."

I confess that I awaited the promised book with mixed feelings. While eager to see this book of my mother's, I thought that what Jean meant

Roxaboxen, sketched from memory by Anna May's stepdaughter Ruth Fleming.

was that my mother had, as an adult, written a book intended for children. I couldn't help fearing that my mother had created precisely the sort of book I hoped to write—and written it better than I could.

Mother was definitely no slouch as an author. When I was in the seventh grade, my sister Ann and I were frustrated by the lack of interesting plays suitable for our marionette theater. Our mother composed a version of "Cinderella"—in verse!—that became the hands-down favorite with both us and our audiences. Mother's eloquence as a writer was casually displayed in everything from personal letters to more formal texts. That she loved to write poems as gifts was something I had enjoyed (and imitated) from my earliest days. She herself had developed this custom in girlhood. After my mother's death, I found a moving poem my grandmother had copied into my mother's "Baby Book," a poem that had been nineteen-year-old Marian's Valentine gift to her. Reading it let me glimpse a vulnerable side of Mother I had never seen. It had never occurred to me that the self-assured parent I remembered might once have wondered—as I certainly had done—if she could quite live up to the hopes and dreams her adored mother had for her.

She lives in a house in my Mother's heart
Where silver pigeons fly
I wish we were not so far apart
My Mother's daughter and I.

Sometimes we meet, I touch her hand
Sometimes she passes by
One grey dawn we talked of death
My Mother's daughter and I.

Tonight we shall talk of lovely things
'Til the Eastern stars are high
And I shall feel we are very good friends
My Mother's daughter and I.

While my mother might not have chosen writing as a profession, she was indeed a skilled writer—and a skilled storyteller. She was, after all, the Mama who told all those wonderful bedtime stories—she certainly could have written the ultimate picture book about Roxaboxen!

But when a large manila envelope arrived from Jean, it did not contain what I expected and half-feared. In the first place, what was inside wasn't actually a book—it was a typed manuscript of the text of a book, a book that had been written and bound by hand in 1916 or 1917. Furthermore, the text's author was not my mother—at least not yet. At the time she wrote *The History of Roxaboxan*, she was simply Marian Doan, a girl of eleven or at most twelve. She wasn't so much as thinking about motherhood—she was totally wrapped up in the fascinating world that she and her friends had created on Roxaboxen.

In addition, what Marian had written was not a picture-book text. Although the spelling was occasionally uncertain (even the spelling of that magic name seemed surprisingly fluid), the style was sophisticated--intended for adult readers as well as for younger ones. The community of Roxaboxen was at that time in full flower, and Marian Doan—its first mayor—had proudly set down a five-chapter history of the town, detailing the features and virtues of this special community. She obviously believed there should be a permanent record—not just for children, but for the whole world—of what she and her friends had created.

In the vivid words of her account, the child Marian suddenly and miraculously stood before me—answering questions that could no longer be put to my adult mother, telling me things I might not even have thought to ask. Later, I learned much from surviving Roxaboxenites, too. I started with my aunts, of course: Jean, Anna May, and Frances. I already knew several other surviving charter members of Roxaboxen: Charles Miller, who had grown up next door to the Doan family; Eleanor Winsor Davis, Marian's closest friend; and Helen Dunbar Lucas, Jean's dearest companion. Through them, I found yet others who had played at Roxaboxen: Estelle Pancrazi Dingus (who still lived in Yuma), Frances Ketcherside McCabe, and Bellamy Abbot. While they all added to my store of information, they agreed that Marian had been Roxaboxen's guiding genius. And thanks to the book she had written some sixteen years before I was conceived, I had

Eva Le Gallienne (Tahe's doll) and Penelopy (Anna May's doll) on Roxaboxen hill, 1918.

Marian close by—as eager to tell me about her creation as I was to listen.

Although I had the typed manuscript Jean had sent me, of course I wondered what had become of the original book my mother had made. No one seemed sure. All three aunts remembered seeing it over the years. In 1976, Marian had lent the book to her sister Anna May who had read from its pages when she taped the text along with her own Roxaboxen memories. Anna May was certain she had promptly returned it, however. My aunt Frances thought Marian might have given the book to her—but diligent searches among her papers produced nothing.

Still, I had the transcribed text. The taped version both confirmed its accuracy and helped me interpret a couple of words about which the spelling might have left me in doubt. What the text offered was richly supplemented by the memories of others who had once played at Roxaboxen. I had the material I needed for my picture book.

When Barbara Cooney began to create the illustrations for that picture book, she wanted to have in her mind's eye the real children who built their town of Roxaboxen. She asked if she might borrow early photos that would help her visualize them as they were during those years. I relayed this request to all the Roxaboxenites and began to search my own household for suitable photos of my mother. I was grateful that I had on my library wall a favorite childhood photo of her, taken just about the time she wrote her book. But I knew that somewhere I had more snapshots from those in Yuma. Finally I remembered where: in a basement file cabinet.

Just after my mother's death, as we children helped my father sort through her things, I had hastily gathered together and taken home some of her materials—photos, a college diary, my mother's "Baby Book," other papers and mementos—thinking that some day I might want to write a biography of my mother. I had never begun the project, though. I hadn't even looked at the materials since that painful time—just placed them in a file for the future. Surely there would be useful photos among them.

I started rummaging through that basement file. Papers. . . letters. . . snapshots. . .and then suddenly, magically, a small book with a delicate sketch of the desert on its cover.

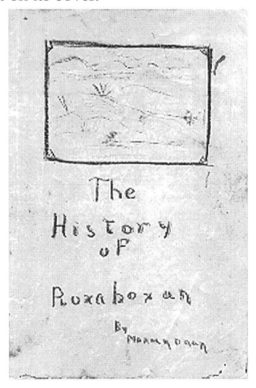

Right in my own house, all the time — the original book.

FOUR

A Portrait of Roxaboxen's Founder and Historian

Introductory Note

I'm not the right person to describe the author of *The History of Roxaboxan* to the world. What is needed is a description not of my mother, but of young Marian Doan—a remarkable girl who had already been transformed to an adult years before I was born. Happily, we do have such a portrait. Around the year 1978, my aunt Frances wrote down her memories of the Yuma childhood she had shared with her sisters—and an entire chapter in these memoirs focuses on the oldest sister, Marian. Thanks to our family tradition of self-publishing, Frances can thus tell us about the girl Marian, the historian of Roxaboxen.

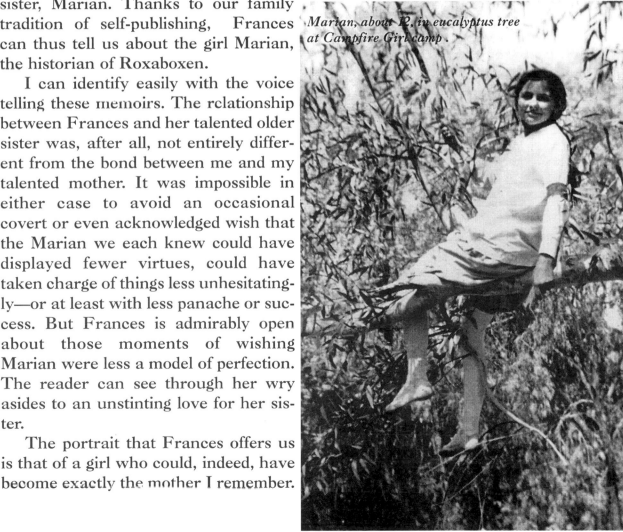

Marian, about 12, in eucalyptus tree at Campfire Girl camp.

I can identify easily with the voice telling these memoirs. The relationship between Frances and her talented older sister was, after all, not entirely different from the bond between me and my talented mother. It was impossible in either case to avoid an occasional covert or even acknowledged wish that the Marian we each knew could have displayed fewer virtues, could have taken charge of things less unhesitatingly—or at least with less panache or success. But Frances is admirably open about those moments of wishing Marian were less a model of perfection. The reader can see through her wry asides to an unstinting love for her sister.

The portrait that Frances offers us is that of a girl who could, indeed, have become exactly the mother I remember.

❧ FIVE ❧

Marian

by Frances Doan Turner
-from her memoir

Memories of Our Childhood

Although each of the four little Doan girls had her moments of glory, or momentary stardom, we three younger ones shone palely in contrast with our really bright luminary, Marian.

One of her earliest triumphs is depicted in a photo postcard, taken July 4, 1912, in Douglas, Arizona, where the young Doan family was living at the period when Arizona's status rose from that of territory to statehood. A float, gaily decorated with flags and bunting and drawn by two stalwart horses, contained young lovelies in white, each representing a state of the union. Perched high above the others sits Marian, portraying "Arizona, the Baby State." She was a beautiful child, and in almost every picture taken of her, her gorgeous dark eyes

D.J.DANIHY MADE MY HARNESS

July 4th 1912   Photo Ed Powell

Marian Irene Doan, 8 months, Silverbell, Arizona, May 18, 1906

arrest the attention.

Marian showed remarkable intellectual facilities and an insatiable interest in the world about her. She was always a bookworm, devouring books like a hungry locust in a corn field. When she was eight and had run low on reading material, she asked May for something to read. The latter, who dearly loved fiction, suggested "Gypsy Breynton," and Marian said, "No, Mama, I don't believe I would care for that. Have you a history of Daniel Boone?"

May Doan, Anna May and Marian circa 1908-09.

"Oh, Marian, you're no child of mine. I believe you will be a blue stocking like Daddy." (John became known among his peers as the "most well-read man in Arizona.") During this same period she asked for a quantity of paper, as she intended to write a book on a s t r o n o m y.

Throughout this account, Frances refers to her parents by their given names.

The book rejected by Marian as too frivolous was, in fact, a novel of 295 pages, written for adults by Elizabeth Stuart Phelps (1844-1911). Offering such a book to an eight-year-old might seem odd today —but some children's books of Marian's time were as long as those for adults and with vocabulary nearly as complicated.

This quotation is taken from May's own entry in Marian's "Baby Book" — but if May said just that she was speaking carelessly, as the phrasing implies that John himself was a "blue stocking" — a phrase meaning a learned, bookish woman. John Doan might well have been both bookish and learned—but as a man he could never be a blue stocking.

Although he himself never had the opportunity to attend college, Marian's father was an early proponent of higher education for Arizona; he fought for it as a state legislator. Frances wrote to Marian in 1970: "I remember typing up material for him in 1931, when I visited at home, regarding a junior college he was proposing, to the legislature, for Yuma. It was too soon, but all his ideas were fine, and he was certainly looking to the future."

May Cargill Doan's own memoirs sketch the situation in somewhat more detail: "When I was in Douglas there was fighting going on in Mexico, the time of the 'Villa' (Pancho), and of course Douglas was just across the line from Mexico. The name of the little Mexican settlement was Agua Prieta. Of course there was not a regular war there, but some skirmishes, and people from Douglas would go down to the line to watch. I remember the Douglas newspaper came out one morning with a drawing (not a real

Unquestionably she acquired <u>this</u> interest from John, who had his children looking through telescopes before they could even read.

In 1913, while the family still lived in Douglas, there was a considerable political upheaval going on in Mexico. May wrote in Marian's "Baby Book," "Just now we are all wondering whether or not we are going to have war with Mexico. Mexico is only eight blocks from where we live so we are more or less interested." (*The understatement of the year.*)

Soon shots were heard from across the border, and curious Americans hovered there to watch the excitement, even though the Douglas papers warned everyone to stay off the streets because of flying bullets. The newspapers in the eastern part of the country exaggerated accounts of the dangers.

John Doan, Frances, Anna May and Marian. Circa January-March 1909

picture) showing lines of citizens from Douglas, many with baby carriages, going toward Agua Prieta, and headlines saying something like this: 'Wires going to Washington begging for protection for Douglas citizens.' Which caused lots of merriment from the readers. Knowing well there was no danger, nor were there baby carriages, but many people did go near the border to see whatever could be seen."

BANDIT VILLA CAUGHT BY CARRANZA TROOPS

FOUND ON HACIENDA AT SAN GERONIMO IN CHIHUA-HUA MOUNTAINS BY SPIES AND LATER CAPTURED BY GENERAL MARQUEZ, WHO CONFIRMS REPORT OFFICIALLY; DECLARED A BANDIT BY CARRANZA AND WILL BE SHOT; NEWS OF CAPTURE AUTHENTIC

(Special to the Morning Sun.)

EL PASO, Jan. 20.—General Villa has been captured by Carranza forces in the mountains of Chihuahua. The first re-

It was shortly after this that we moved from Douglas to Yuma—but not because of the border trouble.

Marian was not long on the Yuma scene before beginning to make her mark. A 1914 news clipping from *The Yuma Examiner* tells of the founding of a girl's club :

GIRLS' CLUB ORGANIZED

Ethel Mayne Shorey and Marian Doan have organized a girls' club, ages 7 to 12. The officers elected are: President, Ethel Mayne Shorey; vice president, Estelle Pancrazi; treasurer, Gloria Robertson; corresponding secretary, Marian Doan; social secretary, Dorothy Moser. The members are: Elizabeth Wallenbeck, Anona Munn, Gladys Wagner, Josephine Pancrazi, Anna May Doan, Marjoria Moser, and Edgar Ingram. The first club meeting will be held at the home of Mrs. E. A. Ingram next Saturday afternoon.

ETHEL MAYNE SHOREY,
President.

May holding Frances. Anna May and Marian standing, left, right. Circa 1909

Frances is too discreet to tell the real story of why the family moved. They had earlier come to Douglas from the town of Silverbell, Arizona (where Marian was born) with considerable reluctance, at the urging of John's father and brother. These two had started a bank in Douglas and wanted John to serve as bookkeeper. Just as May and John were starting to buy a home in Douglas, the bank failed. They lost the home and had to move in with May's parents-in-law—an arrangement that proved far from congenial. May writes in her memoirs of how she tried desperately to earn money without having to leave her children — baking bread to sell, sewing for a friend. Meanwhile, "John was away quite a bit looking for a job in nearby towns, and one day, one of the very happiest days I had had in a long time, there came a wire from an old friend of his, a lawyer in Yuma, named Tom Molloy, and it said, 'Come to Yuma at a hundred a month.' That amount sounds so little now, but in about 1913 it was at least a livable salary . . ."

Inasmuch as Ethel Mayne's father published the *Examiner*, it would seem politic to have had her at the helm of the club. She and Marian were friends in a rather competitive way. I can remember that John ran for the office of Justice of the Peace that first year in Yuma and lost, and when we were on the way to school the morning after the election, we were joined by Ethel Mayne who said, "I see your father lost the election." We felt diminished.

Marian's interests were endless. She spearheaded the formation of Roxaboxen, our town on the hill

John Doan had actually already served as justice of the peace in Silverbell, and as a territorial legislator from Yuma, Arizona — at 23 he was known as the "kid member" of the twentieth Territorial Legislature. He was returned to that office for the twenty-fifth Territorial Legislature from Pima County, and after Arizona became a state, served as representative in the Tenth State Legislature. Following his death, Arizona House Resolution No. 8 (November 17, 1936) cites his record as "a devoted, intense, and intelligent champion of Arizona's development and progress...." Yuma named its high school football field in his honor.

So much for Ethel Mayne

4th Avenue Grammar School, Yuma   *Gloria Robertson, left circle. Marian, right circle.*

across from our home. This was a play area still vividly remembered by
several septagenarians including Estelle Pancrazi Dingus and Eleanor
Winsor Davis. Along with these two friends, Marian, for several years,
entered handwork in the Yuma County Fair. In 1917 she won (class
under fourteen years) first prize for the best dressed doll—said prize was
$5.00 provided by the J. Homer Smith Drug Store. She won second prize
for the best dress, machine-made, and a first prize for best specimen of
button holes. One of the prizes was a year's subscription to *The
Youth's Companion*, a little magazine that was
devoured hungrily by not only herself but
also her three sisters.

She entered poetry contests sponsored by *Woman's Home Companion"* and received one prize for some innocuous verses entitled,

WOMAN'S HOME COMPANION
381 FOURTH AVENUE
NEW YORK

EDITORIAL DEPARTMENT   April 19th, 1917.

Dear Marian:
        Because of your good work in the April Children's Contest, I am sending you under separate cover a little prize which I hope you will like. Try again some time, won't you!

                Sincerely yours,
                        THE CHILDREN'S EDITOR.

*For a poem on "rain drops lullaby"
they sent a box of stationery —*

WOMAN'S HOME COMPANION
381 FOURTH AVENUE
NEW YORK

EDITORIAL DEPARTMENT   June 18, 1918.

Dear Marian:
        It gives me great pleasure to tell you that your verses called "The Bread and Butter Fairies" show so much merit that I am sending you with this a little prize. Try again some time, won't you?

                Your friend,
                        THE CHILDREN'S EDITOR.

Miss Marian Doan,
916 Second Avenue,
Yuma,
Arizona.

No fairy tale of this title seems to exist, but I suspect Marian made a creative adaptation of a tale she liked. The "knocker" would not have been a door knocker, I am sure. In Cornish and Welch folktales, "knockers" are benevolent gnomes dwelling in mines. If treated well, they guide miners to rich veins of ore by tapping in its vicinity. Now, there are no mines for brass — brass is an alloy made of other metals — but Marian may have preferred brass to tin (there is a tale called "The Tin Knocker") and used a little dramatic license.

"Raindrops Lullaby," and another for "The Bread and Butter Fairies."

By 1917, World War I was becoming uppermost in the everyday lives of even those who lived in such a remote spot as Yuma, Arizona. Indeed, World War I, to this day, is almost inseparable in my mind from Marian, who stood out in my view of that momentous period as one of the stars of the "show." Already service for the Red Cross was a paramount activity in the community, and the Camp Fire Girls group, for which Marian was the "reporter," was giving much of its time to Red Cross sewing. A news clipping for 1917 read:

LITTLE GIRL WORKS FOR THE RED CROSS

Sunday afternoon, at the home of Mrs. John Doan, eleven little girls gave a play for the benefit of the Red Cross. Marian Doan wrote the play from a fairy story and drilled the children in their parts.

The play was entitled "The Brass Knocker," and those taking part were: Margaret and Eleanor Winsor, Frances and Allison Ketcherside, Valda Eberhart, Marian, Anna May and Jean Doan, Violet Edwards and Gloria Robertson.

The little girls asked some of their neighbors to come and bring 10 cents each. At the close of the play $2.55 was handed to the secretary of the Red Cross.

Imagine! But where was I, Frances?

Marian had a great capacity for setting goals for herself and following through. May was surprised one day in the spring of 1918, after a period when Marian had been showing particular interest in clothes and had been very particular about how her dresses were made, to hear her say, "Mother, next year make my clothes very plainly, out of plain brown gingham, I think." When May expressed surprise, Marian went on to explain, "Well, you see I want to win the valedictory, so I mean to study hard, and I don't want my mind on clothes!"

Marian had the same single-minded approach to her spending money as to scholastic and other goals. Not for her the frittering away of nickels for candy bars or ice cream cones! She was always saving for a worthwhile purpose. With the coming of World War I, her efforts were directed toward the purchase of War Stamps. These stamps we purchased at twenty-five cents each at the post office and pasted in a War Stamp book, for eventual redemption.

Typical of what we younger ones considered her over-virtuous approach to the patriotic cause was an incident recorded by May in Marian's "Baby Book":

Sunday you were at Daddy's office and he gave you a quarter for ice cream. I said

that evening, "Did you get it?" and you replied, "No, Mother, the post office wasn't open," and smiled at me. Your Daddy was so pleased.

(*I was probably gagging behind the kitchen door.*)

A reasonable question! Frances would have been nine years old at the time. If seven-year-old Jean was included in the play, why was she not?

*World War I had been raging in Europe since Germany declared war — first on Russia, then on France — early in August, 1914. Soon other nations were drawn into the conflict. Sympathy for Belgium had been strong in the United States long before this country finally entered into the war on April 6, 1917. Belgium had fought for motives of sheer heroism and was the only country conquered by the Germans that attempted to organize a resistance movement. For a time ships with food supplies and relief for Belgium were allowed to pass the British blockade, but that blockade was reimposed when it was suspected that the Germans themselves were using the supplies. Over 100,000 Belgian refugees had fled to England, where their adjustment into English life and economy was not easy. Meanwhile, in the Mideast, the Turks had begun massacres of neighboring Armenians — a campaign of such ferocity that today it would be termed "genocide."

World War I marked the first use of toxic gases in warfare, and what Frances remembers about the pur-*

This was also the great Knitting Period. Everyone was knitting, either fashioning articles of gray worsted for the soldiers or knitting colorful squares to be sewed together for blankets for Belgian babies. Belgian babies and starving Armenians were, like the patriotic Marian, synonymous in my thinking with World War I. I never knew why the Armenians were starving, but I remember that if I left food uneaten on my plate at home, I was apt to be reminded of the starving Armenians.

We were also directed to collect tinfoil (such as candy wrappers) and peach seeds. The peach seeds were, or so we understood, to be used for poison gas! At least there has been some progress among some human beings. Marian, who with the rest of us dutifully collected peach seeds for this unhumane purpose, now, nearly sixty years later, would face

14,000 AREMIANS MURDERED BY TURKS

Official Decree Demanded the Wholesale Slaughter; Kurds Assist in Dastardly Work; Children Drowned In Sea

---

ROME, Sept. 1--Fiacomo Gorrini, former Italian consul at Trebizond, who arrived in Rome today, declared that 14,000 Armenian Christians were killed by Turks and Kurds in one massacre at Trebizond. He said:

"The decree, which was published, on June 24, ordered the interment and massacre of Armenians and forms the blackest page in Ottoman history. The result of the publication was carnage on a big and bloody scale. Out of 14,000 Armenians, Catholics and Protestants, residing in Trebizond, only 100 escaped.

"I saw thousands of innocent women and children placed on boats which were capsized in the Black Sea. Thousands of young Armenian women were forcibly converted to Mohammedism. There were suicides without end.

"I shall never forget the scenes of horror I witnessed from June 24 to July 23 when I left.

a firing squad before she would be a party to "Man's inhumanity to man."

We four Doan girls, none of whom were gifted vocally, literally sang our way through the war years. This was the war of the catchy tunes and, with mother at the piano and we four supporting her in song, we belted out "Over There," "It's a Long, Long Way to Tipperary," and various other favorites of the day. "There's a Long, Long Trail A-Winding" was a favorite with us. Refrains still ripple through my memories, little ghosts of the past.

Over there, over there,
Send the word,
send the word, over there
That the Yanks are coming,
the Yanks are coming
The drums rum-tumming
everywhere
So prepare, say a prayer
Send the word, send the
word, to beware
We'll be over, we're coming
over
And we won't be back till
it's over, over there.

The war took on a glamorous aspect for us during the summer of 1918 when we saw some wartime activities

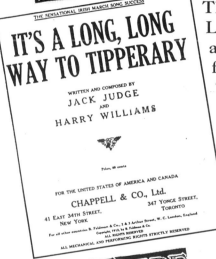

pose of saving peach seeds is probably quite accurate. Although CK or cyanogen chloride (common name: chlorine cyanide) was not fully developed for use until just after that war, when new munition designs allowing its dispersal were created, it would appear that it was under development during the conflict. Peach kernels contain enough cyanogen to poison small children, if several are eaten.

Children of that generation all knew the Germans could be called the Huns, and that their leader was called the Kaiser. They may not have known that Heligoland was a strongly fortified island guarding the entrance to the Kiel Canal, the most important German naval base. The song mentioned by Jean in a letter (p 26) begins, We're on our way to Heligoland to get the Kaiser's goat, In a good old Yankee boat, up the Kiel canal we'll float,…" The name, however, allowed them this delicious opportunity to come within an inch of swearing while singing the song. The Doan girls would never normally have used a word like "hell."

My mother's self-published book "Our Mother's People" let me trace the link be8tween the Doans and the family Marian visited. Kate Morton Cargill, born in 1846, married Harry Stearns. Kate (always called "Aunt Kitty" by May) was May Doan's paternal aunt, and her children would be May's cousins. By the account here, her son Robert had a wife named Mabel and a daughter Elise.

At that time the Pacific fleet (which was later moved to Pearl Harbor) was based at San Pedro, the harbor for Los Angeles. It would appear that oversight of the military activity at the port was primarily in the hands of the Army. The unnamed "colonel" mentioned with awe later in the account of Marian's visit must have been a regimental commander from nearby Ft. MacArthur — an important Army base for many years, closed in 1974.

She went by train, the common means of long distance travel in that era. Even during the period of World War II, when I was a child, travel by air had not yet become common.

through Marian's eyes—or, rather, as we saw them portrayed through her letters written from San Pedro, California, where she spent a month with relatives. May's cousin, Robert Stearns, was serving as a Christian Science Wartime Minister for the armed services. He and his wife and little daughter had taken an apartment for the summer at San Pedro, where there was much military activity as the warships prepared to sail from that harbor.

Although Marian had spoken up five months earlier for a plain brown gingham wardrobe for the 1918-19 school year, she left Yuma for San Pedro in early August 1918, with much less austere clothing. As May phrased it:

We had so much fun getting you ready. Made you a pretty pongee dress with featherstitching, in red, and bloomers of pongee also, and a lovely new red hair ribbon. White stockings and white socks also, and tennis slippers and very pretty shoes—black patent leather with white kid tops. You made a smock of buff linen, smocked in black, all by yourself. You have a new red sweater and cap also. These, with your middy skirt, two white middies, two brown ginghams, and a white dress, complete your wardrobe. Anna May and Frances ran blue ribbons through your gowns. Daddy bought you a pretty tan purse for your money and tickets. You have your dark green coat and straw hat to wear, and your yellow tam-o'-shanter put in your suitcase.

In recognition of all the preparations that went into her trip, Marian was conscientious in writing home and keeping her family informed as to her adventures. The first evening in San Pedro she and the Stearns family had supper by the wharf and saw the ships; one battleship was just ready to sail. She reported that it was so successfully camouflaged that it looked like a little yacht with two sails! In retrospect one wonders what reaction the German Navy would have had on spotting a yacht with two sails in mid-ocean in war-time.

She wrote of Cousin Bob going to Richmond for a few days and said she, Cousin Mabel, and Elise would miss him as he did most of the housework. She, Marian, couldn't imagine John doing housework and wrote, "Daddy, if you ever happen to go to Richmond, I think we could manage." She also reported:

Cousin Bob is very good looking and has twenty-three ties in the bathroom; as I counted them carefully. I took a hot bath; you just turn on a faucet marked "hot" and you have all the warm water you want!

Marian's expenses on her trip. Written on the back of the Woman's War Relief Program on the following page.

For a family to eat in a restaurant in those days would have been a rare event. It is likely that this supper was a picnic prepared by Mrs. Stearns.

According to William Oleson at the Maritime Museum of San Pedro, the use of camouflage for ships only began in 1918 — so what Marian observed may have been a pioneering effort. It was forbidden in wartime to photograph camouflaged ships, so we have no evidence that would let us guess whether the Germans would have found the disguise as effective as Marian did.

This would have been Richmond, California.

She wrote enthusiastically of going to a review of the soldiers and sailors and said the music was grand. The music of the military bands must, indeed, have been very stirring to a little girl accustomed only to those small concerts given by Yuma local talent in the summer on the grammar school lawn.

Every Saturday, at nine o'clock, she and her hosts went to "Muster," and this she liked best of all. "It gives you such a *thrill*, Mother." Her knitting continued unabated, and she knitted trench-caps for the soldiers, among other things. Her letters were full of mention of aeroplanes, biplanes, submarines, and other things pretty unfamiliar to her three sisters. They, of course, were fascinated by her faithful accounts.

She remained in San Pedro well into September. A letter from her hostess to May, dated September 8,

The program from the concert Marian attended in Los Angeles.

THE STAGE WOMEN'S WAR RELIEF

PRESENTS

To The Boys of the Naval Base

Tuesday, August 20, 1918

The following PROGRAM staged by
WALLACE REID

1.............OVERTURE
By the Naval Base Band

2............."I'm Going to Be a Leader in the Navy"
Sung by Margy Carson
Accompanied by Prof. Kerwin

3.............Katherine Melville Crocker
Accompanied by Marjorie Hicks

4.............HUGH FAY
in "Camouflage"

5.............CELESTE CONANT
(Tuneful Tale-Teller)

6.............LILA LEE

7.............OVERTURE
Naval Base Band

8.............MARY PICKFORD

9.............KATHLEEN CLIFFORD

10.............BEBE DANIELS

11.............WELLINGTON CROSS

12.............BOB ALBRIGHT

S. W. W. R. Representative . . Lillian Brockwell

Courtesies acknowledged to
THE FAMOUS PLAYERS-LASKY CORPORATION

Hollywood Citizen Print

A biplane similar to what Marian would have seen.

1918, says:

> *The Colonel has taken a great fancy to Marian. He picks her out to speak to and actually unbended enough to wave to her today. He and his family have been most formal with us until this morning when they all unbent and were <u>almost</u> jolly. . . . Now, my dear, if all your daughters are as charming as <u>this</u> one they are most welcome to visit us at anytime.*

Marian's charm was undeniable, and even I, who tended to be somewhat jealous of her, recognized her special quality. It is just as well that I never visited the Stearns family, except in the company of my sisters and mother, because I would have fallen far short of the mark.

As the finale to her visit in San Pedro, the Saturday before she left she wrote, "This afternoon was the most eventful of all. I viewed three hydroplanes, four submarines, the San Pedro docks, and several hundred yachts from the prow of a camouflaged ship." Her cousin Bob later took her over the ship. When I read her letter, I envisioned her reviewing the "troops" like

That the colonel loosened his normal stiff reserve doesn't mean that we should imagine that he waved to Marian from the reviewing stand! After the troops were dismissed, there must have been a certain socializing among family members who had gathered to observe the military inspection, and the colonel might have lingered to participate. Cousin Mabel's surprise at the "unbending" of the colonel and his family is understandable. In the Army I remember from my childhood (I was brought up in a military family), rank was indeed a significant factor even in social situations — and maintaining one's place in the hierarchy was most important to some. When in 1952, my father was — as a colonel — the Military Attache at the American Embassy in Ecuador, my mother was roundly scolded by the wife of a visiting general for failing to give that ranking spouse the place due her (I think the one on the right?) in the Embassy limousine.

The first Oz book by L. Frank Baum was published in 1900. It is not clear when the Doan family first discovered these works, but perhaps they were introduced to them by Eleanor Winsor. The Winsor family's extensive personal library was an important supplement to the Doan's own overflowing shelves. In another chapter of her memoirs, Frances writes of how the Doan girls "often trekked to the Winsor establishment, not only to play with the young Winsors but to borrow their books. Before the Carnegie Library was established in the city park, the Winsor library was a chief source of reading material for us...The Winsor library was chiefly housed in an outbuilding that must have been originally designed as a cooler or ice house. It was thick-walled and cool even in the summer. Mr. Winsor, who probably bought the property from a farmer, lined the walls of this outbuilding with shelving, and here were to be found books of all ages."

The Oz books were Doan favorites, and that love has continued down the family line. I recently sent

royalty.

To us she was another "Dorothy" in a veritable land of Oz, so foreign were her experiences to anything with which we were familiar! Her letters were magic carpets that lifted us, temporarily anyway, out of the drabness of the long, hot August days, spent mostly inside the Doan bungalow where the droning of the electric fans provided a hypnotic illusion of coolness.

We had all four visited in Los Angeles two summers previously, so we could envision to some extent Marian's surroundings. That was a halcyon period for Southern California. The skies were clear and sparkling, with no hint of smog to dim the horizon. Acres of orange groves perfumed the air. No mammoth shopping centers or housing developments had begun to encroach on the countryside, and the seven story downtown Bullocks in Los Angeles was considered a high-rise. The glamour of the movie colony was on an ascending spiral.

Of course, during Marian's stay in San Pedro, we at home wrote pretty regularly to her. This typewritten letter from little Jean, who was 7 and not a terrific speller, must have afforded her amusement rather than nostalgia.

```
        Dear marian ,

I am sending you a letter ,
I meen I am sending you a rock and I panted a fase .
Thank you for the red cross ,
I out to cut out  a white pees of rag and soe it n
on the rag ,
and play we are a red cross nerces ,
I am so glad you whint to the beech ,

        privet ,

pealeas write me a letter and tell me what you
wrote in mothers letter ,
I know I ot not to say it ,

I hope you are having a good time ,
the riben of the tipwriter wus brokent and
dady chist fixetd it ,
anna may tite 5 stripes on t_e fan ,
and whin you tern the fan on the string
blose and blose ,
miss stap poot that cloth on the peanoe ,
and it looks so pretty ,
I know how to play a little of where do we go
frome here ,
and I am on my way to hellogo land fo get the
cisers go ,
and  I know a hole lot of peeses ,
whin you come home whith  teris I see mother will
play *e are on my way to helogo land ,
I will have to herry cos in a minot mothers
going to male the letters ,
I am feeling fine ,
I dident go swiming yet ,

I will have to close ,

you lovenly freand

        Jean ,
```

Marian once wrote back, "Sometimes I get a little homesick, and then I take out my letters and read them and get more homesick."

To this day Jean writhes at the resurrection of some of her early letters.

While in Los Angeles for the final days of her vacation, Marian was feted by May's girlhood friends and went to the Orpheum and Morosco, those splendid rococco theaters—then in their hey-day—and to the Bimini Baths.

And then home by Southern Pacific to dry, hot, dusty Yuma, home to the grey bungalow with the scarred front steps and carpetless floors, all of which were in such contrast to her brief sojourn in "marble halls." She came home enriched with new experiences and widening vistas of the world and with a greater appreciation of the social graces. But after all it was *home* to which she returned, home to the arms of her welcoming family. The camaraderie of the four sisters, the warmth of her own family circle, the challenge of the school year which she hoped to climax with the attainment of the valedictory...these, after all, were the warp and woof of her life.

During the ensuing school year, whether or not dressed in brown gingham, Marian proved well able to keep herself from being distracted in her pursuit of academic honors. Her report cards during this final year in the grammar school are studded with neat rows of "E's" for Excellence.

my own complete Oz collection off to my oldest grandchildren — but find I miss having it around.

May's mother had died when she was ten. Two years later, her father moved with May and her siblings from Poughkeepsie, New York, to Brookhurst— the name of a quite luxurious ranch situated between Los Angeles and Anaheim. They lived there for ten idyllic years. In her memoirs May describes fondly the "lovely, large house" with its six bedrooms, its vine-covered veranda, its many bookcases filled with books, its tennis court and croquet ground. Her father, a risk-taker with expensive tastes, eventually lost the ranch and took employment in Yuma, where the family adapted to a much more simple life. May was by that time 22 years old, and quickly secured a job as a bookkeeper — a role she learned on the job. In her memoirs, she notes demurely: "A young man named John Doan helped me a lot." Although she spent the rest of her life in Arizona, May continued many of the California friendships she had made during her years at

Throughout that year, Marian carried on with her unflagging support of the war effort. There is still extant a yellowed clipping of a long article which appeared in the Yuma daily paper, "Victory Pledges We Must Fulfill," by Marian Doan. The article is lengthy but well written, especially for a child of thirteen. The last paragraph impresses me with the thought and research she must have given it:

The armistice that ended the battles of World War I was signed on November 11, 1918 — but American soldiers remained in Europe after that date. The Treaty of Versailles was not signed until June 28, 1919.

VICTORY PLEDGES WE MUST FULFILL

By Marian Doan

It is a simple thing to sign our pledges on the spur of the moment, but we should give more thought their fulfillment. We should fully estimate the amⁿ give| It is wrⁿ⁻ ⁱᵒⁱ we thir⁻ ⁻⁻⁻ ⁻ rew of us ⁻ ⁻⁻ lose money.

I would like to say something about the cause to which our money goes. In other wars, the influences of the home had to stop at the soldier's front gate. Now the home follows the flag clear up to the farthest French village where our boys are booked. During the war it did not stop until our soldiers had cheer in the front-line trench. When the camps are near large cities, the soldiers naturally want to spend their furloughs in town. If you have read the histories of other wars, you find that the soldier's leisure is almost as dangerous as the enemy. The seven organizations we subscribe to, provide decent and inexpensive places for them to sleep and eat. At the depot, he finds an Information booth conducted by the War Camp Community Service. Here he can get the names of libraries, churches, and museums. There is little room for lonliness in the cheery huts, sup-

Although the final words can no longer be read on the clipping, they were: "Supported partly by the dollars we pledge. . . ."

Another small clipping reads:

The eighth grade has organized themselves into a war relief society and voted to keep one Belgian child for one year. Also each member pledged to buy a thrift stamp a day. There are 40 members in the class. George Steiger was elected president; Marion Doan, secretary; and Gertrude Glasser, treasurer.

If my memory serves me correctly, thrift stamps were ten cents each. I don't know how many of the forty eighth-graders followed through with a thrift-stamp-a-day, but without doubt Marian did.

Marian's determined race for the valedictorian's laurels was a neck-and-neck contest with her great friend and neighbor, Gloria Robertson. Gloria was a petite youngster whose heavily fringed, large, grey eyes were almost a match with Marian's dark orbs. Fortunately, their rivalry was friendly. An example of their commitment to academics was the fact that the two of them were among four eighth-graders who had a perfect attendance record for the year. (Three fifth-graders who had similar records did not include young Frances.)

When the final day came for the announcement of the valedictory, there was only a fraction of a point between Marian and Gloria. Marian got the valedictory and Gloria the salutatory.

Marian was a picture of grace and beauty as she appeared on the stage of the Gandolpho Theater on commencement night—except for her shoes! May had made her a dream of a dress, fashioned of white organdy, so fine it had a silken sheen. There were six rows of ruffles on the skirt, a beruffled sash that tied in the back with a big bow, a soft cowl collar and sleeves that flared below the elbow in ruffled cascades. Her dark hair, parted at one side and tied with a huge white bow, hung in curls down her back. She wore white stockings—but her feet were encased not in dainty slippers appropriate to the rest of her costume, but in what we

This same pattern was repeated four years later when the two girls graduated from high school. The academic rivalry did not affect the warmth of their friendship. Later on, Marian was married in a veil lent her by Gloria.

siblings thought were the most outlandish footgear she could have chosen. She was, about that time, entering her phase of selecting wholly comfortable and sensible attire—and she had sent away for a pair of white buckskin shoes, *ankle high*, that fit no category we could name. They resembled present-day basketball shoes. Fortunately, they were dimmed by the shadow of the footlights, which focused on her beaming hair and shining raiment.

The infamous white shoes?

Our neighbor, Mrs. J.B. Dunbar, who had studied elocution at one period, had coached her in the delivery of her address. This much-thumbed sheet has many penciled underlines, and, in the margin, such reminders as "Relax," "Lower voice," "Break," "Intimate, personal."

She delivered her address with great aplomb, and her family sat basking in reflected glory.

SIX

Roxaboxen
The First Written History

A facsimile edition of Marian Doan's *The History of Roxaboxan* is included with this publication—but although her handwriting is in general legible, her spelling is not always conventional, so it seems appropriate to offer a typed transcription. I have added notes to provide background. Although reading the text just as it was written is a delight, for full appreciation of certain parts of Marian's account the reader may wish to have a more detailed view of what was happening to the Doan family—and to Yuma—during the timespan of the history.

When the meaning of a word may be in doubt because of spelling, I have included an interpretation of that word. I confess it was only Anna May's confident reading of the text that let me realize that the word transcribed as *close*?—which had puzzled me in the typescript I first received—was a misreading of *drose*, which I might in any case have failed to recognize as a creative spelling of *drowse*!

The Mr. Jenkins to whom Marian's book is dedicated was an Episcopalian minister of whom the family was especially fond. Although he later moved to Tucson, he and the Doans stayed in touch over a period of many years.

The dates on the inside cover are written in my mother's adult hand, and obviously indicate her own estimate, made in later years, of the period within which the book was written. My own belief is that the actual composition took place in the first of the two years named—perhaps at the end of the summer of 1916—when Marian was still eleven years old, about to turn twelve. The last actual historical events recorded are, after all, the accounts of the Roxaboxen wars that took place late that summer. Had the text been written

Marian, age 12.

much later, I believe her spelling would have been more sure. It is surprising how flexible she is about the spelling of the memorable place name itself. The very first page offers three different choices!

I would judge that some of the street names given on her map, which surely are those she herself chose, evolved over time into ones that seemed more natural to the group playing on the hill. All my Roxaboxen informants remember as "Main Street" what her map calls "Roxaboxen Rode." (Yuma's own main downtown street was called simply "Main Street," and to imitate this straight forward label would have been tempting.) "Stickery Street," however vivid a name, was mentioned by no one. That her book uses what may have been early forms of the street names offers further reason to think that the book was probably published while the settlement of Roxaboxen was still relatively young.

Jean, when she sent me her typescript, also estimated the date of writing as being early in the community's history. She noted that she herself makes no appearance on the book's pages. Although she was still a bit young to be included when the settlement was founded in 1915, within two years she and her friend Helen had joined the older children on Roxaboxen. Had the book been written in 1917, it seems reasonable that they would have been mentioned.

That Marian's vocabulary and style are sophisticated does not imply that she need have been older than eleven at the time her book was written. This young author was a voracious reader, and the books for children of her generation were challenging ones.

And now we come to the heart of this volume: a faithful facsimile of Marian's self-published book.

SEVEN

The
History
of
ROXABOXAN

by Marian Doan

The Facsimile

The History
oF
Roxaboxan

By
Marian Doan

Affectionally dedicated
to Mr. J. R. Jenkins.

Date
1916 — 1917?

The History of Roxaboxen
Chapter I

Roxaboxen - this name is derived from two words, rocks and box, of which it is stated the town is composed. It may be said at the first that no one knows the origin of Roxaboxen. Playing on the hill may have begun, years ago before the present owners ever heard of it. Many signs of civilization have been found which cannot be accounted for, such as carved initials, buried tobacco tins of rocks and other treasures. The site of Roxaboxen is on one end of a large hill, one side of which is cut into a sharp precipice past which flows the river* Rode. The other side branches off into another small hill while the end is another steep bluff in which are some of the richest minerals ever known. On the eastern side is a spot of no small prominence, this is Fort Irene. It is a large rock protruding from the slope, which is at least eight feet square, on each side of which are two giant ocotillos. This historic spot has probably been used

Road

in every battle fought upon the hill
The bluff on the western side has often
been used in playing, the small caves
being of greatest use. Many rich mines
are situated at the end with cabins for
the miners to reside in. Both silver and
gold can be found here. The silver at
first when first taken from the mines,
looks like a white powder but after being
mixed with water can be molded into
any desired shape. The gold is a yellow
clay and if too dry has to be dampened
in order to shape it. Beside these two important minerals there are iron and copper,
rubies and emeralds besides many other
nameless precious stones. As we have
fully described the city the next chapter
will be about its first course in history.

Chapter II

One day in 1915, five children ascended the steep grade by the Rode river and began to plan a house. They were Artemus Lane, Valda Eberhard, Buster Eberhard, Marian Doan and Frances Doan. It was early in the morning and they set about carrying rocks and marking off boundaries. At that time the country was infested by bears and rattlesnakes and they had many thrilling adventures. To add to their inconveniences cyclones were frequent and they often had to take shelter in the caves by the riverside. In spite of these difficultys their dwellings gradually grew. A large cactus in Valda Eberhard's room was chopped away, remains of which are still standing. In various way the houses grew to apartment when it was suggested that each own a separate home. At first houses were only one room when the idea was welcomed but they found more room was needed.

to Marian Doan; Buster Eberhard and Artemus Lane who were in partnership moved to the other side of the hill selling the land they had previously owned. Many extra buildings sprang up, a courthouse, a jail, a museum and several stores. The roads were enlarged as new settlers came. Among them were Lois Goodwin, Eleanor and Margaret Winsor, Beatrice an Byorn McInnis and Anna McDoan. This period represented the first growth of Roxaloxan and was of wonderful importance. The next chapter describes the off and on between months of calm after the Doans went to Somerton.

Chapter III

The end of the last chapter mentioned the Doans departure to Somerton. After this Roxaboxen was neglected though the foundations were so strong it was none the worst. Wind and rain could make no impression on solid rock. It was in August 1915 when the arrival of the Doans who were visiting Mrs Shanesy awakened interest. This was one of the greatest revivals in history. Play was taken up enthusiastically and for days the city limits grew. A grocery store and two icecream parlors started and many new homes built. After the Doans left Marian Oan still stayed two weeks longer so interest was not abated until school began which is the greatest enemy of Roxaboxen. Finally on Jan. 22, 1916 came the flood which was a great help to Roxaboxen in this way. Mr Moore died and this meant the Doans would stay in Yuma.

However unfortunately their house is a block away from Roxaboxen and they found some other way to occupy their time in a small strip of mesa land beside their house. Also another town had been started in back of Roxaboxen called* Jan Mooreflood. But Roxaboxen waited patiently for she knew they would come back to her in the end and so they did as the next chapter proves.

* Sometimes called Sandywaren

Chapter V

When the Sloans came back from their summer vacation, they found a surprise awaiting them for Mr. Doan had moved into the house they had first occupied when coming to Yuma, right across the street from Roxaboxen. This meant a new revival but it happened this time it was in a different way. And that way was - battles. A war arose between the boys and girls. Those on the boys side were bandits, while the girls were girl scouts. The Girl Scout headquarters were at Fort Irene which has already been mentioned and the boys were stationed at a shed which belonged to Mr. Stitt. The girls had a great advantage over the boys as their fort was in a better position but soldiers could hide in the boys fort without being seen. The girl scouts were - Margeret Winsor, Marian Doan, Eleanor Winsor, Beatrice MᶜInnis, Anna May Doan, Frances Downs

Frances Ritcherside and Frances Yeniam
The bandits were Artemus Sane, Charl
Miller, Louis Goodwin Buster Eberhar
Paulie and Jackie Rooney and Omar Johns
These two parties fought many batt
and every other day the hills rang with
shouts. When school began play once
more calmed and Poxabuxen began to dr
But it will rise again and why the last
chapter will show.

Chapter II

Roxaboxen is one of the finest playgrounds for children I have ever seen. No wagons or carts go through it, no one can dispute the right of land. It has every advantage, the children who play on it are true to it, it will never be deserted. The clifts, the rocks, the bushes all proclaim its freedom. Its mines are always a source of entertainment, its valleys not less so and the town of overwhelming delight. The mysterious Treasures it holds give more joy than clifts of gold and silver, the honey of the ocotillo tastes better than the daintiest we can buy. On Roxaboxen imaginary dinners satisfy hunger as well as real ones. No one covets the possessions of another.

real sin is unknown. Looking for missing goods is only a keen diversion instead of something to cultivate suspicion and hate. Nothing ever loses its charm and its citizens will forever cry "Hurrah for Pixabrien.

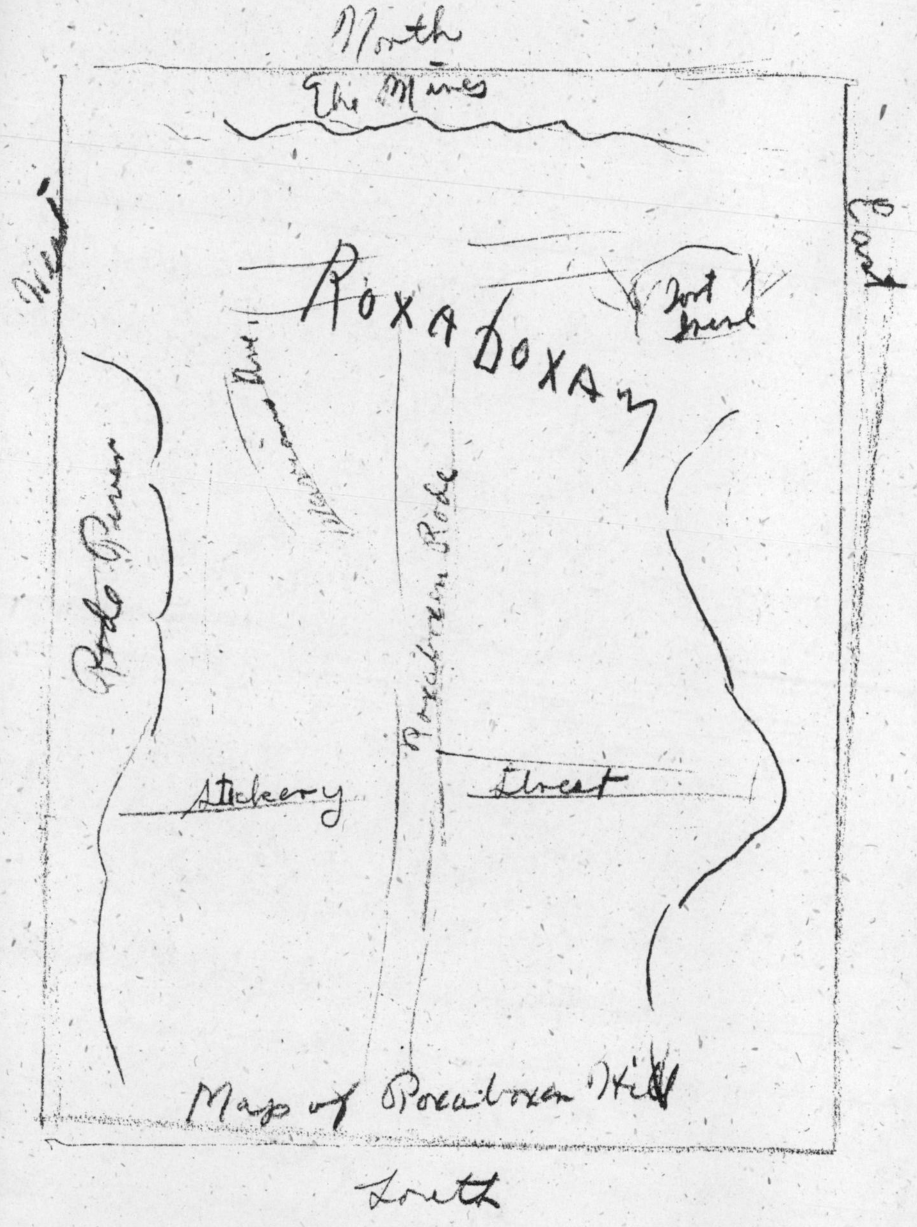

North

The Mines

R O X A D O X A n

Fort General

Middletown Ave.

Robb River

Poradoxa Road

Stokery   Street

Maps of Pocadoxa Hill

South

West

East

ISBN 1-888842-09-1

†*Irene was Marian's middle name. In her taped remarks, Anna May noted that the name of the fort, and Marian Avenue (the street curving west from Roxaboxen Road or Main Street) "indicate that our sister Marian. . .hid behind no false modesty."*

*Road (Marian's own asterisk)
†The remainder of the manuscript makes it clear that the unpaved road in front of the Doan house, a road that at that time curved into Eighth Street rather than making a sharp corner, had been transformed in imagination into a river.*

Chapter I

Roxaboxan — this name is derived from two words, rocks and box, of which it is stated the town is composed. It may be said at the first that no one knows the origin of Roxaboxen. Playing on the hill may have begun years ago before the present owners ever heard of it. Many signs of civilization have been found which cannot be accounted for, such as carved initials, buried tobacco tins of rocks and other treasures. The site of Roxaboxon is on one end of a large hill, one side of which is cut into a sharp precipice past which flows the river *Rode.† The other side branches off into another small hill while at the end is another steep bluff in which are some of the richest minerals ever known. On the eastern side is a spot of no small prominence, this is Fort Irene.† It is a large rock protruding from the slope which is at least eight feet square, on each side of which are two giant ocotillos. This historic spot has probably been used in every battle fought upon the hill. The bluff on the western side has often been used in playing, the small caves being of greatest use. Many rich mines are situated at the end with cabins for the miners to reside in. Both silver and gold can be found here. The silver at first when first taken from the mines, looks like a white powder but after being mixed with water can be molded into any desired shape. The gold is a yellow clay and if too dry has to be dampened in order to shape it. Besides these two important minerals there are iron and copper, rubies and emeralds besides many other nameless precious stones. As we have fully discribed the city the next chapter will be about its first course in history.

Anna May and Marian reading. Circa 1916.

†*At that time the Eberhard family lived in the house just south of that occupied by the Doans. Later, this house became the residence of the family of Charles Miller.*

Chapter II

One day in 1915, five children acended the steep grade by the Rode river and began to plan a house. They were Artemus Lane, Valda Eberhard, Buster Eberhard,† Marian Doan and Frances Doan. It was early in the morning and they set about carreing rocks and marking off boundaries. At that time the country was infested by bears and rattlesnakes and they had many thrilling adventures. To add to their inconvenience cyclones were frequent and they often had to take shelter in the caves by the riverside. In spite of these difficultys their dwellings gradually grew. A large cactus in Valda Eberhard's room was chopped away, remains of which are still standing. In various way the houses grew to apartments when it was suggested that each own a separate home. At first houses were only one room when the idea was welcomed but they found more room was needed. So Marian Doan, Buster Eberhard and Artemus Lane who were in partnership moved to the other side of the hill selling the land they had previously owned. Many extra buildings sprang up, a courthouse, a jail, a museum and several stores. The roads were enlarged as new settlers came. Among them were Loie† Goodwin, Eleanor and Margaret Winsor, Beatrice an Byorn† McInnis and Anna May Doan. This period represented the first growth of Roxaboxan and was of wonderful importance. The next chapter describes the offs and ons between months of calm after the Doans went to Somerton.†

†*Byron*

†*Louie*

†*The job that had permitted the Doans to move back to Yuma from Douglas (see notes on page fifteen to Frances Doan's memoir of Marian as a child) was welcome but not ideal. May Doan's memoirs tell of the move to Somerton: "In August of 1915, John was offered a position in Somerton, a town about twelve miles from Yuma. A Mr. Caruthers was opening a bank there and asked John to go out as manager. I was glad that none of the family had anything to do with this bank, and Mr. Caruthers had plenty of money back of him....I must confess that when I saw the tent house that was to be home with the two double beds and a table and the large iron wood-stove that I was to cook on, and realized the heat we would have to endure, my heart sank, but no matter how difficult it seemed it couldn't be anything like as hard as it had been in Douglas and the summer turned out to be a pleasant one after all....The women of Somerton insisted that the afternoon we moved down, [that] I walk up and down the one street and call on everyone. I must say that tale was not true but I did meet them all just as soon as I could." The one photo I have of my grandmother from this period shows her in an improvised fancy dress — perhaps as a Turkish princess? No circumstances could keep May Doan from building a happy life, and I suspect she herself was the organizer of whatever masquerade gala was involved.*

John Doan did manage to secure another small tent for cooking and eating, "and it was a good thing too, because we had to put everything on the beds in order to cook on the iron stove and then put everything on table and stove in order to go to bed."

Domestic life in early Arizona may have been carried on under difficult circumstances, but ladies were still expected to keep themselves and their children neatly dressed in the styles of the period--even if those styles were more suitable for colder climates. Mrs. Waldron, a friend from Silverbell, with her infant Robert on the left; Marian and May on the right. June 1906. Can you imagine dressing like that in the heat of the Arizona desert? JUNE! My grandmother reminded me often: "Horses sweat, and men perspire--ladies merely glow." Ladies must have glowed a lot in those days.

† *Catherine O'Conner was an Irish girl from Chicago who had worked for May Doan's father when Andrew Cargill was running the Southern Pacific Hotel in Yuma. Catherine O'Conner had then married J.H. Shanssey (this unusual spelling was confirmed by newspaper items from that era), former mayor of Yuma, and moved to a house across the street from Stuart Cargill. May's brother Stuart Cargill was a carpenter, and while the Doans were in Douglas, he had begun building a house across from Roxaboxen. During the first two weeks after the Doan's return to Yuma from Douglas, the Doans slept in the nearly-finished house but ate at Catherine Shanssey's. May confesses in her memoirs that she had at first been doubtful about Catherine's marriage to a man more than twice her age: "When Catherine told us that she was going to marry old Mayor Shanssey, we felt a little fearful. We liked both of them, but there was such a difference in their ages and upbringing. But the marriage was most successful, and she took splendid care of him until his death." Catherine Shanssey became a favorite with the entire Doan family; she was called "Aunt Catherine" by the Doan girls. The Yuma Sun noted a visit by Mrs. J.H. Shanssey and Mrs. A.T. Pancrazi to Mrs. John Doan of Somerton on June 25, 1915, and a return visit by Mrs. Doan to Mrs. Shanssey. We can assume that a later visit to their hospitable Yuma friend included the entire family and that they remained at the Shanssey home for some days. Marian's delight in being back in Yuma is clear from her account, and surely inspired her hostess to encourage that she stay on after the other Doans returned to Somerton.*

Chapter III

The end of the last chapter mentioned the Doans departure to Somerton. After this Roxaboxen was neglected though the foundations were so strong it was none the worst. Wind and rain could make no impression on solid rock. It was in August 1915 when the arrival of the Doans who were visiting Mrs. Shanesy awakened interest.† This was one of the greatest revivals in history. Play was taken up enthusiasticly and for days the city limits grew. A grocery store and two ice cream parlors started and many new homes built. After the Doans left Marian Doan still stayed two weeks longer so interest was not abated until school began, which is the greatest enemy of Roxaboxen.† Finally on Jan. 22, 1916 came the flood which was a great help to Roxaboxen in this way. Mr. Moore died and this meant the Doans would stay in Yuma.† However unfortunately their house was a block away from Roxaboxen and they found some other way to occupy their time in a small strip of mesa land beside their house. Also another town had been started in back of Roxaboxen called *Jan Mooreflood.† But Roxaboxen waited patiently for she knew they would come back to her in the end and so they did as the next chapter proves.

*Sometimes called Sandywaxen (*Marian's own footnote*)

†*This perception that school was in competition with Roxaboxen for the children's time helps explain the otherwise puzzling fact that Roxaboxen — for all its range of civic amenities — never had a school. Marian had a genuine appreciation for the value of education — but the demands of formal education, when viewed from the perspective of Roxaboxen, might take on a different cast.*

†*The flood threatened Somerton as well. May Doan's memoirs tell the story:* "The Gila River and the Colorado were high at the same time and the levee broke and Yuma streets were flooded, even had to have boats going up and down Main St. — and Stuart, in Yuma, was afraid that the river would also flood Somerton. So he drove down to take the children and me to town, John had to stay with the bank. I remember that Stuart was hurrying us off and I was throwing into a sheet the things I felt I must save and do you know I put John's dress suit and a dress suit of Father Judge's into that sheet when the only use they were to have was in the H.S. Drama Club. I expect I left out many things we would have really needed. However, the flood did not reach Somerton and so we came back a few days later....But we <u>were</u> to move to Yuma after all, as the Yuma Title Co. manager, a Mr. Moore, got very excited when the flood came and in hurrying to get valuable papers out of the safe, he had a heart attack and died. Then Mrs. Michelson, who now owned the Title Co. after her husband's death, asked John to come to town and take the manager's position. It was work that John knew so well and at a better salary and the Yuma school was much better for the children, so he accepted at once and Mr. Caruthers put someone else in charge of the bank. Stuart's house was rented then, so John got a place for us on Orange Ave., opposite the Ketchersides."

The Mr. Moore that May mentions so casually was, I should add, mayor of Yuma at the time of his death. The Ketcherside home stood on the corner of 8th Street and Orange (the latter running parallel to 2nd Ave., just one block to the west). Frances Ketcherside—another Roxaboxenite—and Frances Doan were best friends. That they shared the same name was made less confusing than it might have been by the fact that Frances Doan was known by her family nickname of "Tahe." Frances Doan Turner and Frances Ketcherside McCabe remained close to the end of their lives.

†"*Jan Mooreflood*" *was transcribed as* "*Dan Mooreflood*" *in the typescript of Marian's book that I first received from Jean,* and during the period I was writing my own text, my aunts were convinced that "Dan" was the first name of the mayor who died in the flood. Even after Marian's book was discovered with its unmistakable "Jan," Anna May believed she had corrected that to "Dan" when reading, and the tape somehow distorted her voice to make the word sound like "Jan!" I thought that research in Yuma newspapers from the period of the flood would clarify whether Jan or Dan was the first name of the mayor — but it only compounded my confusion. The man's name was given both as Charles H. Moore and Charles M. Moore—but Charles it definitely was. Neither middle initial offered a potential for a nickname of Jan or Dan. I belatedly realize that my aunts were unlikely, in fact, to have been familiar with the first name of the man who had been mayor during their childhood. In those days children did not call adults by first names, nor would parents have so referred to an adult when talking to a child. Almost certainly "Dan" represents an error in typing at the time the book was first transcribed. Taken by all of us years later as a man's name, it suggested a "false memory" that would explain its appearance as part of the invented place-name.

Only recently have I realized that Marian gives us the clue to interpretation of her place-name—by specifying that the flood occurred in January! I'm confident that Jan Mooreflood was named in honor of the JANuary flood that killed Mr. Moore.

I wish Marian had been equally helpful in hinting at the roots of her alternate name for this suburb of Roxaboxen, which may have been situated on the east side of the hill. The "sandy" part is easy—but I have no idea what "wax" was involved.

†*May Doan described this vacation a visit to May's sister Irene Foster in her memoirs. While John stayed working in the heat of Yuma, she and the girls went to California to visit Irene and Alf Foster. "We had such a happy time at Foster's. It was a chicken ranch but there was an orchard with many fruit trees, and the orchard was on a road from San Francisco to Santa Cruz and there was a lot of traffic. I wanted to learn to milk and so did the children. While we had been on Orange Ave., our next door neighbor had had a cow. One day he had to be away and John promised to milk the cow for him. I was very astonished and said, 'But, John, you can't milk a cow!!' He insisted he could, so I immediately asked all the neighbors over to see him do it, still very much in doubt that he really could milk. So at six when John was ready to milk, several neighbors were hanging over the fence, and I was the most surprised one of them all, as John did a beautiful job. So Alf would let the children and me take turns learning to milk, and one afternoon when a car was passing, he heard someone say, 'Why, there are two — no, three people milking one cow!'"*

†*As May notes in her memoirs, her brother had by that time sold the house he had built — but they continued to call it "Stuart's house" even though they now rented it from its new owner.*

Chapter IV

When the Doans came back from their summer vacation† they found a surprise awaiting them for Mr. Doan had moved into the house they had first occupied when coming to Yuma, right across the street from Roxaboxen.† This meant a new revival but it happend this time it was in a different way. And that way was — battles. A war arose between the boys and girls.† Those on the boys side were bandits, while the girls were girl scouts. The Girl Scout headquarters were at Fort Irene which has already been mentioned and the boys were stationed at a shed† which belonged to Mr. Stitt. The girls had a great advantage over the boys as their fort was in a better position but soliers could hide in the boys fort without being seen. The girl scouts were — Margaret Winsor, Marian Doan, Eleanor Winsor, Beatrice McInnis, Anna May Doan, Frances Doan, Frances Ketcherside and Frances Yeman. The bandits were Artemus Lane, Charles Miller,† Louie Goodwin, Buster Eberhard, Paulie and Jackie Rooney and Omar Johnson.† These two parties fought many battles and every other day the hills rang with shouts.† When school began play once more calmed and Roxaboxen began to drose. But it will rise again and why the last chapter will tell.

†*The Miller family had been the Doan's neighbors in Somerton and had moved to Yuma about the same time the Doans returned to that town, moving into the house just to the south of theirs. Charles, who was Marian's age, went through high school with her. He was an ideal "boy next door" — and continued over the years to be as close as a brother to all the Doan girls.*

†*Although in the picture book I elevated the Rooney brothers to the list of initial settlers, I at the same time changed Jackie's name to Jamie, for the sake of the softer consonant. I confess I now regret that decision. I do not regret, however, another liberty with the truth I took: naming Charles as one of Roxaboxen's first settlers. Had he lived in Yuma at the time, he certainly would have been climbing Roxaboxen together with those listed in Marian's first chapter.*

†*It is not surprising that the children should have had war on their minds. World War I was at this time raging in Europe, and this nation's papers were full of speculation that the United States might soon leave its neutral stance to join the allies who were battling Germany. The Yuma newspapers also reflected — often even more vividly — concern that the United States might be drawn into war with Mexico. Headlines about Villa and his "bandits" often overshadowed those about aggressive acts by the Germans. Not until the days immediately before this country's actual entrance into World War I did Yuma headlines dealing with what was going on in Europe take clear precedence over those describing the violence threatening to spill over from Mexico. This tilt in the balance of concern should not be too surprising, nor should we be surprised that the aggressors on Roxaboxen were "bandits" rather than "Huns." Europe was very far from Yuma; Mexico only a few miles away.*

†*This shed was located near the south end of the hill. Further south, at the end of the block, was the house where Gloria Robertson lived — at that time the only house on that side of the street.*

Anna May, Frances,
Marian, and Jean.
circa 1916

†*It's a miracle they weren't truly bloody battles. The primary weapons were swords, for which the children used long, stiff wands of ocotillo — bristling over their entire length with closely-spaced sharp thorns! It is clear from the enthusiastic accounts of veterans of these wars that the battles were lively indeed — yet the warriors seem to have avoided doing major damage to one another.*

Chapter V

Roxaboxen is one of the finest playgrounds for children I have ever seen. No wagons or carts go through it, no one can despute the right of land. It has every advantage, the children who play on it are true to it, it will never be deserted. The clifts, the rocks, the bushes all proclaim its freedom. Its mines are always a source of entertainment, its valleys not less so and the town of overwhelming delight. The mysterious treasures it hides give more joy than clifts of gold and silver, the honey of the ocotillo tastes better than the choicest we can buy. On Roxaboxen, imaginary dinners satisfy hunger as well as real ones. No one covets the possesions of another, real sin is unknown. Looking for missing goods is only a knew diversion instead of something to cultivate suspeicion and hate. Nothing ever loses its charm and its citizens will forever cry, "Hurrah for Roxaboxen.

EIGHT

Marian Grows Up

MARIAN DOAN
1927

The sketch given in Frances's memoir, and the words of Marian's own work, tell us a great deal about the young author. But the reader may want to know what became of Marian as the years passed—and some of that later history relates to Roxaboxen, so it seems fair to sketch it here.

While Marian and her friends began creating Roxaboxen in 1915, a seventeen-year-old named Herb Enderton was attending classes at Tempe Normal School in Tempe, Arizona—a teacher-training institution that has since evolved into Arizona State University. At that time, "TNS" had a five-year course for grammar school graduates. Herb, with a year of high school behind him, had entered in 1912 as a second-year student. A serious, unsophisticated lad with blue eyes and dark hair parted on the side, Herb had grown up in isolated mining camps where he and his brother were often the only children. At Tempe, he worked for his room and board in the role of janitor

Herb Enderton 1915.

of the boys' dormitory; now and then he worked in the dining hall as a table waiter. After his graduation, he taught school for a brief period. But the United States—which had at first stayed neutral—finally entered World War I in 1917, and he didn't want to be a slacker. Not long after twelve-year old Marian returned from her visit to San Pedro, Herb went to Tucson and enlisted in the Army. After the war ended, unsure of his vocation as a teacher, Herb resumed his studies—this time in engineering, at the University of Arizona at Tucson. In the spring of 1919, near the end of his first term, he

Marian about the same age as when she traveled to San Pedro

Charles Miller, with a buggy whip. Few photos of Charles are available, and this is a pre-Roxaboxen pose. Still, his role in introducing Marian and Herb demands that he have a place on this page. The day after they met, Charles hand-carried Herb's first letter to Marian (see next page) from Fortuna into Yuma.

was offered an appointment to the United States Military Academy at West Point, New York—a splendid educational opportunity he accepted without hesitation.

In the summer of 1923, Charles Miller was working at the Fortuna gold mine near Yuma. The mining engineer in charge of the Fortuna, one Bert Enderton, was visited that summer by his twenty-five-year-old son Herb—a new lieutenant in the U.S. Army who had just graduated from West Point. Herb Enderton and Charles Miller soon became good friends.

Charles at the time was infatuated with Gloria Robertson—she of the large grey eyes with long lashes, described in Frances's essay. Herb was curious to meet this local charmer of whom Charles was always talking, and Charles was happy to show her off. Gloria came to Fortuna on a picnic with her mother—and she brought along her neighbor and friend, Marian. Only seventeen that summer, Marian had just graduated from high school. Many years later, Marian still loved to tease her husband Herb that his first words on being presented to the two girls were,

Herb. Westpoint 1923.

"Which is Gloria?" As my father ruefully noted in his own memoirs (we are obviously a family of memoir-writers!), that was "...admittedly not a diplomatic way to open a conversation with one's future wife!"

However awkward the initial meeting, by the end of the day brown eyes had eclipsed grey ones for Herb, and his habitual shyness was beginning to dissolve. That night, after the girls and Mrs. Robertson had left the mines and returned to Yuma, the young lieutenant found himself writing a letter to Marian,

1

Fortuna Mine
July 22, 1923.

Dear Marian,

It is now eleven forty-five, and before I finish it will be past midnight. It's a poor time for a working man(?) to be writing a letter, isn't it! But I wanted to drop you a note for Charles to take in tomorrow. Don't ask me the purpose

2

of the note, for I'll be unable to tell you. And too, it's near midnight, and one grows less responsible for his actions as the small hours approach. Oh Marian, we had a real rain last night, a rain that actually made muddy puddles of water in the road between here and the Mess Hall. But the water soon dried, and tonight

3

one would not know, except for the cooled air, that it had ever rained. The water goes as quickly as it comes here. But anyway, during the few short hours that the water was on the ground, the poor frog up by the Mess Hall had a chance to learn to swim. It has been so dry since the little fellow's birth that his croak had become a dry rasping sound similar to the noise made by a dull rip saw. I hope that the moisture will help to lubricate his vocal organs!

4

When the rain started I had to move in from my bed on the hill. I spent the remainder of the night in our bunkhouse. As you probably remember, the foot of the swing is a foot or more lower than the head, and one takes chances of falling out, but after you get used to the swaying of the porch roof it makes a fairly good bed. By the way, did you find the pictures, Marian? I'm sure we left them at the house. Must say "Good night", or rather it is now "Good morning." Marian.

Sincerely, Herb.

The note was the beginning of an unwavering courtship—one that was obliged to continue for six years, as Herb adjusted to Army life and Marian realized her dream of going to college. At first she and her family were uncertain such higher education would be possible—but she won a scholarship that permitted her to attend the University of Arizona. Marian made Tucson headlines as she enrolled; she had tested higher than any entering freshman on the intelligence test used by the University at that time. In 1928, she graduated Phi Beta Kappa. She and Herb were already formally engaged and would most certainly have married by then—but just at that point the Army assigned Herb to Madrid, Spain, for a year,

in an assignment that allowed no place for a wife. Still, sometimes reality can be almost as good as fairy tales; I think my mother

MISS DOAN EXCEPTION TO RULE THAT MEN OF "U" MOST INTELLIGENT

Women's Leadership in Scholarship Result of Closer Application, Psychologist of University Says; Results of Tests

This Diploma Certifies that Marian Doan is a member of the Honor Society **Phi Kappa Phi** by election of the Chapter in University of Arizona She is hereby granted all the honors and privileges pertaining to the Society

President of Chapter
Secretary General
President General

UNIVERSITY·OF·ARIZONA·
GREETING·
M·THESE·LETTERS·SHALL·COME·
BY·VIRTVE·OF·THE·AVTHORITY·VESTED·IN·IT·BY·LAW·AND·ON·THE·REC·OMMENDATION·OF·THE·VNIVERSITY·FACVLTY·DOES·HEREBY·CONFER·ON·
MARION·DOAN
Freshman Honorable Mention—Sophomore Honors—Junior Honors
WHO·HAS·SATISFACTORILY·COMPLETED·THE·STVDIES·PRESCRIBED·THEREFOR·
THE·DEGREE·OF·
BACHELOR·OF·SCIENCE·IN·EDUCATION
WITH·ALL·THE·RIGHTS·PRIVILEGES·AND·HONORS·THERETO·APPERTAINING·
IN·WITNESS·WHEREOF·THE·SEAL·OF·THE·VNIVERSITY·IS·HERETO·AFFIXED·
DONE·AT·TVCSON·ARIZONA·THIS· FIRST ·DAY·OF· JVNE
·IN·THE·YEAR·OF·OVR·LORD·ONE·THOVSAND·NINE·HVNDRED·AND·TWENTY·SEVEN

CHANCELLOR
SECRETARY·OF·THE·BOARD
GOVERNOR·OF·ARIZONA
PRESIDENT·OF·THE·VNIVERSITY
SECRETARY·OF·THE·FACVLTY

Herb and Marian's wedding, 1929.

came as close to living happily ever after as life allows. In 1929, when Herb returned from Spain, Marian Doan at last married the only man she had ever loved, and the two of them lived happily until her death fifty years later. Their letters to one another during the long separation occasioned by World War II (letters which my f a t h e r retyped and bound for each of his four children after our mother's death in

Anna May Doan, Jean Doan and Frances Turner as bridesmaids for Herb and Marian's wedding, 1929.

1980) are a luminous testimony to their mutual devotion.

As a family we had to weather the years of World War II, not a brief conflict we could easily sing our way through. Even in times of peace, a military life involves the stresses connected with moving to a new post every year or so— again and again a new town, new house, new schools, new network of friends and activities. The adult Marian was a model Army wife and mother. She surrounded us with love when our father was in battle on the other side of the world. By her cheerful example, she helped us children learn to be at ease with the challenges and serendipities of the gypsy life we led before and after the war. But she was more than wife and mother. During much of her

LADIES' HOME JOURNAL
The Curtis Publishing Company
Loring A. Schuler, Editor
PHILADELPHIA

July 16, 1930

Mrs. Herbert B. Enderton
West Point, New York

My dear Mrs. Enderton:

We thoroughly enjoyed reading your article entitled "For the Dumb-bell Cook." You have touched upon some of the points that we have considered weak in our general instructions to new homemakers - some that we are planning to emphasize during the coming months.

A check will be sent to you shortly.

Very truly yours,

Lita Bane

Editor, Department of
The Modern Homemaker

LB:MM

THE UNITED STATES FIELD ARTILLERY ASSOCIATION
THE FIELD ARTILLERY JOURNAL
WASHINGTON, D. C.

March 25, 1937.

They published.

Mrs. Herbert Enderton,
Fort D. A. Russell,
Marfa, Texas.

Dear Mrs. Enderton:

Your article on MARIA was a delight to read, but extremely dubious of publication. I'll have to sleep on it. A lady wrote me one about Schofield—and submitted it to the higher-ups. I never saw it. That gives me pause.

You see my job is—or at least I think it ought to be—to present the readers with problems they are capable of solving. There are a few incorrigible hunters, like myself, who would like to go to Maria regardless. What chance would we have if our wives read your story? The lady who wrote the Schofield story told me she had read but one Journal issue in her life—and that one made her mad. But I can see that desired—with certain reservations.

For instance, it begins to look like our feminine contingent would eventually develop an editorial policy for us.

I'll write you again about this article, and in the meantime will save it for chuckling purposes, if I may. Your pen deserves a wide audience, and I hope will get it, even if not here.

Sincerely,
Michael V. Gannon,
Captain, FA.,
Editor.

life, she was also a dedicated teacher. Always, she was a citizen who took civic and social responsibilities seriously, a paragon of intellectual curiosity and diligence. Could we have expected less of the young Marian that Frances describes?

The little girl who caught the fancy of the colonel's family in 1918 San Pedro was by the end of her life a colonel's lady herself. The child who made crossing the road into an adventure had traveled the world. In 1946, after the war ended, we had joined my father in Europe for a year. There, Marian entertained princes and princesses at her table with the same grace with which she had once presided at Roxaboxen tea parties. Roxaboxen, after all, let you practice all the skills needed for anything in life.

Even after both she and Herb had in theory retired, Marian was an activist for so many worthy causes that my father finally posted above the phone a small sign saying simply, "NO." Not that he expected her to change her ways, of course—he just wanted her to remember, when the next caller asked for Marian's leadership on behalf of some urgent endeavor, that it was possible to say something other than "yes."

Friendships forged on Roxaboxen were deep ones. Not surprisingly, most of the Roxaboxenites who survived into adulthood stayed in touch over time and distance. Not all of them lived to adulthood, unfortunately. Buster and Valda Eberhardt both died of typhoid in June 1921.

Article about the work Marian Enderton did in Ecuador while a part of the "Damas Americanas," the "American Ladies.

Marian Enderton at an orphanage in Quito, Ecuador..

(Frances also had typhoid fever during her sophomore year of high school but recovered.) Eleanor Winsor Davis remained my mother's close friend in spite of all the miles that the nomadic nature of Army life put between them. Helen Dunbar Lucas and my aunt Jean, who built their houses together on a side street of Roxaboxen, are still best friends. Charles, Eleanor, Helen—they were there with Marian's three sisters in Rancho Bernardo, California in 1979, when my parents celebrated their golden wedding anniversary.

I should add that not only my mother but every Roxaboxenite I came to know was in adult life an interesting, articulate, and good person. I

can't help thinking that what they created together on that hill—the shared and independent play, the comfortable silences and the long conversations—had something to do with it. They could learn leadership and cooperation; they could develop initiative and independence and imagination. The ever-deepening bonds of friendship taught them much about loyalty and generosity of spirit.

I wish every child could have a Roxaboxen.

Marian Doan Enderton
1977

Roxaboxen
The Picture Book

Working with the materials provided by Marian's book and by surviving Roxaboxenites, I was able to write what became the text for the picture book since published by Lothrop, Lee & Shepard.

The project was a long time in development. Interviewing started with phone calls—but soon more was needed. In April of 1986, I visited California to interview my aunts Anna May and Frances in person. There were letters exchanged with Eleanor and Charles and soon with other surviving Roxaboxenites to whom they and my aunts led me. All this took time—and digesting the rich material took yet more time. There were stories to visualize and hand-drawn maps to ponder. There were memories of my own to pull to the light. I've had places like Roxaboxen, too, and I needed to remember how that felt.

I had still not put one word to paper when Larry and I left for Europe that next summer. I should explain that my husband is a theoretical physicist whose work often takes him to other countries—either for international conferences and meetings or for visits that allow exchange of ideas with colleagues abroad. I love being able to tag along. These professional travels offer such fascinating experiences that we seldom take time for a true vacation—but the summer of 1986 was different. Larry and I both love mountains. In 1984, we had moved from

Alice McLerran, photographed on Roxaboxen in the spring of 1987 by her aunt Frances Doan Turner.

Seattle, Washington (breathtaking Mt. Rainier was close to that city, as were other peaks of the Cascades and the Olympics), to Fermilab, a national accelerator laboratory set in the cornfields west of Chicago. Two years on the flat plains had left us hungry for time together on mountain trails. We had reserved a full eleven days of our summer trip as personal time, intending to spend it hiking in the Bavarian Alps.

When the time for this vacation arrived, we headed south from Frankfurt, Germany, to Garmisch, where we meant to start our hike. As our train pulled into the station at Garmisch, it began to rain. It continued to rain. It rained without real pause for the first ten of those eleven vacation days.

Hiking was clearly out of the question; we spent those ten days holed up in a tiny rented apartment. Larry played a lot of solitaire, hoped for a break in the weather and tried to contain his frustration. I, on the other hand, was perfectly happy. I had at last finished digesting the material; I had the telling of my story roughly mapped out in my head. The text for *Roxaboxen* was finally ready to be written, and this was my chance to do it! I regretted not having brought our notebook computer from Frankfurt—but less sophisticated writing materials were readily available. By the time those ten days were over the text had gone through draft after handwritten draft and was already polished to something near its final form.

So it was during ten days of rain, in mountains far from Yuma, that the desert town of Roxaboxen entered into a new revival. Although my story was composed in the age of computers, by chance it was—like Marian's own book—written first by hand.

I was pleased enough with the finished text, but at first I hesitated to submit it for publication. I couldn't see how an artist could find any way to illustrate it successfully. I thought that what I had written might perhaps be a poem to share with those who already knew and loved Roxaboxen, rather than the basis of a picture book. After all, how could anyone draw imagination? Sensible writer-friends firmly reminded me that that difficulty was the publisher's problem, not mine—so I sent the manuscript off to Lothrop.

Editors Dinah Stevenson and Dorothy Briley knew an artist capable of drawing imagination: Barbara Cooney.

Normally artist and author never meet, but this book was a true collaboration. Barbara devoured all my source materials. In

Barbara Cooney, photographed at La Valencia Hotel in La Jolla, California. She, Tahe, and Alice met there for lunch, and then aunt and artist set out for Yuma. Spring 1988.

conversation with me, she explored why I had wanted to write the book; how I hoped it could affect the reader. She visited Roxaboxen—first with Frances, later alone. She collected and studied photos showing the children who had played there, the neighborhood as it

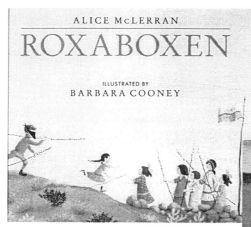

looked then. She delved deeply enough to do what I myself had attempted to do when I was preparing to write the text She learned so much about Roxaboxen that in her imagination she could become a child playing on that hill.

You might thus say that Barbara Cooney and I have played together on Roxaboxen. The children who actually built that town together in Yuma were friends for life— bonded by the depth of the experiences they had shared, by their fondness for, and pride in the creation of their joined imaginations. I like to think that Barbara and I are now so linked.

Reviewers and readers love Barbara's glowing pictures, but to my mind the finest compliment comes from Helen Dunbar Lucas—close friend of my youngest aunt, Jean. Helen long ago built her house next to Jean's, on the east slope of Roxaboxen. "It's hard to believe she wasn't playing there with us," Helen said of Barbara Cooney. "She drew it just the way it felt."

Not the way it looked, mind you, the way it felt. That's harder.

The book almost immediately appeared in Japanese translation; the Scholastic Book Club made it available in

O should explain here Barbara Cooney's dedication of her work in *ROXABOXEN*, which reads, "To my Roxaboxen guide, Tahe." Tahe is the nickname by which Frances has been known since early childhood. In this book, I have followed the example of my aunt--who refers to herself as "Frances" in her memoirs--so as to avoid confusion. Actually, all her family and friends would normally refer to her by her family nickname. How did she get such a nickname? I can tell you, although the story may not seem a satisfying explanation. When Jean was just learning to talk, "Tahe," was how she pronounced "Frances."

both in English and Spanish versions. Viking-Penguin published a paperback edition. Spoken Arts produced a beautifully-read video of the book.

There was immediate interest in the book in Russia. ("*We* played that way!" exclaimed the first Russian friend to read the story.) Sergei Sukharev, a skilled literary translator from St. Petersburg, made an excellent translation that was broadcast in 1989 on "Goodnight, Children," a popular radio show for Moscow children. It seemed that a Russian edition of the book would be com-

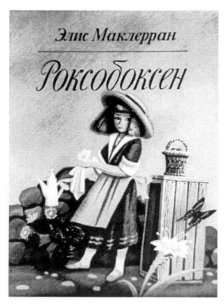

Cover and one of the illustrations by Galina Lavrenko for the never-published Russian edition.

ing out, using new illustrations by Galina Lavrenko. But in those early days of glastnost, the rising prices of paper first drove one would-be publisher out of business, then made the project impossible for the next one interested in undertaking it.

Back in the U.S., various educational editions and uses have appeared. IBM's Eduquest developed a CD-ROM using the book for its *Stories and More* series. The popularity of the book shows no sign of waning. My Russian friends urge me to explore again the possibility of an edition there. I'm not sure the end of uses and adaptations of the book here or elsewhere has yet been reached.

But the picture book has been successful in a deeper way than can be counted in copies printed or subsidiary rights sold. It has inspired children to build Roxaboxens of their own; it has drawn adults back to memories of their own magic places. I'll always be proud of this book.

Roxaboxen
The Play

In April of 1996, I heard from William Morrow & Co. (parent company of the house that publishes *Roxaboxen*) that a playwright wanted to adapt the book for the stage. I was flattered but puzzled. The history recounted in the picture book is a quiet one. The only event of obvious dramatic potential is the war between the boys and the girls—and one could hardly emphasize that without distorting the nature of the tale.

Although Morrow actually owned the dramatic rights to the story, they graciously left approval of the project in my hands. I read the letter and materials that Richard Rosen had sent from San Antonio, Texas. In addition to being an active playwright, Richard is the Executive Director of the Magik Theatre, a non-profit children's theater serving that community. His letter ended: "*Roxaboxen* appeals to me because it is a simple, poetic call for all of us to value the imagination of childhood. It's like a memory poem which is relevant to every generation. Our theatre attempts to present works which stimulate communication within a family. I believe this piece could do just that."

Richard Rosen with his Roxaboxen T-shirt , a gift from Jean.

In spite of my doubts, how could I not be favorably inclined? I called Richard Rosen immediately, and we spent a long time on the telephone in our first conversation. That conversation left me reassured that he understood and respected the spirit of the story, that he indeed cared about nurturing imagination as much as I did. If any playwright could work the miracle that would let Roxaboxen live again on the stage, he seemed a good choice. He himself said candidly that he didn't know how he'd go about doing it—but he wanted permission to try. By the end of the conversation, I was happy to grant that permission. I trusted him.

Over the next months, we talked more. He patiently pulled from me

material about Roxaboxen that had inspired me without finding any
actual place in my story. I told him, for example, how when my aunt
Frances was a young mother, she had gone back to visit the hill and stood
looking down at the house where she had spent her childhood—a house
that now belonged to others. She had experienced, she told me, a sudden
feeling that if she could only run down the slopes of Roxaboxen fast
enough, by the time she got to the foot of the hill she'd be a child again.
The house across the road would once more be her's, and she could simply run across the street and be home.

Roxaboxen did encourage one to
think that anything is possible.

I remember explaining to Richard,
also, how I believed that the wars on
Roxaboxen were echoes of what was
going on in the adult world at the time.
Roxaboxen was built, after all, during
World War I.

I told him a lot of disconnected
things. I had no idea how he was going
to use any of it.

The play was scheduled to premiere
in September of 1996. That July, during
a month in the U.S. between the visits

White stones.
Thorny plants.
Wooden boxes.
The stuff of
any old desert.
With a child's
imagination,
These forgotten
things become.
a house a fort
a town.

The Magik Theatre's announcement of
the play.

to Europe we were making as part of my husband's sabbatical year,
Richard Rosen and I talked once more. It was our last chance to do so—
I wouldn't be back in this country until two days before the play opened.
To my dismay, I discovered he hadn't yet begun a first draft; he still want-
ed to draw more material out of me. "Richard," I said, "I'm afraid I don't
know what more I can give you."

But then I remembered: I had with me a xeroxed facsimile of
Marian's *History of Roxaboxan*, a book I always carry to share when I
visit schools. I described the book and offered to send it to him. A few
days later we left for Denmark. During the rest of that busy summer, I
tried not to worry about how the play was developing. Richard will do it
somehow, I told myself.

I wasn't going to miss the premiere, of course—but I flew to San
Antonio not knowing what to expect. My first reassurance came when I
entered the small theater and saw the set. It was as right as Barbara
Cooney's pictures had been. Bebe Canales Inkley—formally the presi-

dent of the theater's board of directors, informally fairy godmother, patient gofer, and everything useful in between—had even managed to locate some real ocotillo to complete it.

Although I am sure every child in the audience was already familiar with the picture book, the play was prefaced by the director's reading of it once again, sharing the pictures with the children seated before him. In that intimate theater, this bold stroke worked. Once the story was over, he asked softly: "Would you like to see Roxaboxen come to life?"

Dave Cortez (from left), Monica Hester and Ruben Ortega-Young help bring the Magik Theater production of ROXABOXEN to life.

"Yeahhhh," was the eager response.

"Okay," he told them, "you have to help. I want you all to whisper three times, in a very magic way: 'Hurrah for Roxaboxen!'"

As the lights dimmed, every child whispered the phrase: once, twice, three times. Recognizing the last words of Marian's book, I could not keep the tears from my eyes. I knew then that everything was going to be all right.

And it was.

Actually, my original misgivings weren't unreasonable ones. A straight adaptation of my book almost certainly would not have worked. But Richard's play was not such an adaptation—it was a unique creation that used the picture book, used Marian Doan's book, used everything I had told him.

It used things that came from neither source—but Richard's intuition that they were right for the play was flawless. Neither my book nor Marian's offers any real explanation of how the black pebbles that became the money of Roxaboxen happened to be buried on the hill in a tin box—but I am sure that Marian herself would have approved the imaginative interpretation offered by the children in the play, an interpretation climaxed by a rousing "Pirates in the Sand" song.

Richard Rosen had never seen Frances's essay on Marian, the memoir offered here as a portrait of the young author. He had no way of knowing how the song "Over There" had echoed in my aunt's memory as she looked back on those years when Roxaboxen was at its height.

Nonetheless, that song echoes in the play as well. The play links Roxaboxen warfare—casually, naturally—to unease about World War I, the real conflict going on at the time. Exhausted from their mock battles, the children rest together at the crest of the hill, talking about whether they'd ever want to fight in a real war. The death of the lizard that has become special to the children is discovered near the end of this conversation. As the children bury their dead lizard, the girls begin to sing "Amazing Grace." The boys softly sing lines from "Over There"—and the two tunes blend together in bittersweet counterpoint.

Material from the two books was woven together by the playwright's creative imagination to make a seamless new work of art. The play uses text from both lavishly, but probably more ideas from my mother's book than from my own. To be sure, an Alice/Author character is onstage throughout as narrator and observer, but Marian's book offers the dramatic possibilities that my own story never suggests—and Richard's staging lets the audience feel the thrill of encountering imaginary cyclones and bears!

Jean with cast and crew of the play. 1996

Weaving different source materials together gives the play a depth, a poignance, that a mere adaptation could never have. As the play nears its end, Marian is writing in her notebook, and the actors who play the children recite in turns the lines that she is writing: the final chapter of her *History*, a poem to the permanence of what they have built. They finish the poem and shout triumphantly together, "Hurrah for Roxaboxen!" But school is beginning; classes call them from their play—the children must leave Roxaboxen. Marian is the last to go, looking back wistfully at her town. The Alice/Author character then gradually walks toward the top of the platform that represents the crest of the hill, reciting text taken from the last page of my own book—lines about the passage of time and the endurance of memory. As she does so, the children from Roxaboxen walk slowly out and up to take their places with her: older now, ghosts from another time and place.

"My" character then says:

> *As the world gets smaller, and cities grow more crowded, Roxaboxen will always be there—an open space for the imagination. I go back often. I stand on top of the hill and look down. Standing with me are…(as she names each child in turn, the actor playing that character says his or her own name in unison with her)…and all the others who created this dream city. I want to run down the hill holding hands with all of them. Somehow in my heart, I know that if we do, we can defeat time—and, when we reach the bottom, we will all be children again.*

Frances's vision, made universal!

They do run down together: laughing, the adult "ghosts" becoming children once more. As they reach the bottom, they begin singing a transformation of a haunting "House of Jewels" song that has been used earlier in the play. Richard Rosen's words and Roger Underwood's music here become a hymn to the capacity that lets all of us create "imaginary havens for the best and worst of days." On the stage, the child Marian stands hand in hand with an adult Alice, singing of the power of imagination. That is, of course, exactly what she and I were both celebrating in our books—although the books themselves were written some seventy-five years apart. The magic of theater allows me to watch myself and my child-mother side by side, hands linked, singing our shared song in unison.

I had been right to trust Richard Rosen so utterly. He had understood both Marian's book and my own. He had understood Frances's vision, back when as a young mother she stood on the hill and was moved by its magic. The music that Roger Underwood composed and wove throughout the action of the play was an unexpected bonus. Evocative and moving, it set the mood in wordless scenes, magnified the power of the lyrics. Thanks to these two, Roxaboxen has come to life yet once more: this time as a play.

Jean with the four actresses portraying Marian (Monica Hester), Frances (Heather Huston), Little Jean (Martha Dickman), and Anna May (Becky Miller).

ELEVEN

Roxaboxen
The Place Itself

I remember clearly the first time I actually saw Roxaboxen, although I'm not sure just how old I was—perhaps ten. My grandmother had moved from the house in which she and my grandfather had raised their girls, but still lived in Yuma. We were visiting her there, and my mother was driving us four children—my sister Ann, my brothers Herbert and Don, and me—somewhere. As our car was passing a hill, she pointed out the window. "That's Roxaboxen," she told us.

I recall vividly the rush of excitement mixed with disappointment, as I craned to see it better. Excitement because I knew it was a magic place; disappointment because it looked so ordinary.

Barbara Cooney surely felt much the same at her first view of the hill, which by that time had suffered neglect and damage. The note at the end of *Roxaboxen* described what she saw: "a small tan hill dotted with stones and rocks, a scattering of desert plants, and now lots of broken glass and an old car chassis."

Still, although the open slopes adjacent to Roxaboxen have shrunk— buildings have encroached on these lower, more level portions—the hill itself has continued to stand, defying the development that is the normal fate of most vacant land in towns.

I now know a surprising amount about that hill, even about its formation long before Marian and her friends played there. Fred Croxen, a geologist who teaches at Arizona Western College, became interested in the hill—and gave a lecture on "The Geology of Roxaboxen" to a group meeting at a church just across the street from the hill. From a tape of that lecture sent me by the church's pastor, I learned Fort Irene is an out-

Roxaboxen in 1997, shortly before commencement of restoration.

crop of a mass of very old granite, and that this durable stone underlies the entire hill. This granite, formed some 1.4 billion years ago, represents some of the oldest exposed rock in North America! Roxaboxen granite, which can also be viewed on the "cliffs" facing the intersection of 2nd Avenue and 8th street, is a handsome stone with a pinkish cast, enlivened by the glint of mica.

When I last visited Yuma, Fred himself filled in an important part of his lecture that was lost as the tape was reversed—identification of the special peb

Detail of Roxaboxen from the mural "Yuma County Past and Present" by Joel Zerega and Leon Myron. Property of the Yuma County Library District.

bles used as money on Roxaboxen. The traditional money of Roxaboxen, smooth black pebbles that always seemed like river pebbles, are in fact just that. They are signature pebbles that mark an ancient course of the Colorado River. There are two major rivers in the Yuma area—the Gila and the Colorado—and these distinctive black pebbles are associated with the latter. The stone of which they are composed is chert from old limestone beds; such black chert can be viewed near the lower levels of the Grand Canyon. Pieces carried down by the rushing waters of the Colorado were smoothed by tumbling to form the smooth pebbles the children discovered on Roxaboxen.

New houses on Roxaboxen, 1997.

Yuma lies at the apex of the delta of the Colorado. Over time that river has deposited many tons of material in the area, carved and recarved its bed in different paths through the silt, sand, and stones it earlier carried down. River terraces have been uplifted over the eons and become hills. While today the Colorado normally flows tranquilly through Yuma—tamed by the dams, diminished by irrigation, often seeming more stream than river—the black pebbles speak of a time when it approached the sea with more grandeur.

Fred mentioned the inclusions of even more ancient fragments of rock within the basic granite and of streaks of more recent feldspar and quartz that probably represent events some seventy-three million years ago. At that time the area was subjected to pressure and molten rock intruded, leaving these streamers. So while Marian may be correct that no one knows the origin of Roxaboxen, we do know enough to see the hill as geologically interesting, a record in stone of dramatic events over vast reaches of time—a suitable setting for its historic settlement.

In the years after Marian and her friends moved away, Roxaboxen continued to wait. For many years the hill was as I describe it at the end of my picture book—traces of the town the children had made still visible. Stones do not move spontaneously, after all.

The Doan house in Yuma in 1997.

But then a contractor bought the hill. He decided it was time something profitable was built there. I'm told he ordered a bulldozer to scrape the hill away, so as to create a flat building site. The bulldozer certainly did some damage. The vegetation and lines of stone, all the softer parts of the surface, were indeed scraped away. By the time I went back around 1982, the top was flat and hard. Little remained of the soft deposits once left by the Colorado. There was no more ocotillo to provide thorny swords to young warriors. Instead of rounded, translucent bits of desert glass, there were broken beer bottles.

Yet the hill itself remained. The bulldozer had been stopped by Fort Irene and all that lay beneath that "spot of no small prominence." Granite is a hard stone. Roxaboxen could not be scraped away.

The failure of his first plan didn't stop the contractor, who persisted in his intention to build. Perhaps it is only local rumor, but I was told he asked the City of Yuma for a permit to blast the hill! Fortunately, the fact that Roxaboxen stands close to houses would have made such an idea impossible. Roxaboxen's core of granite saved her by making construction impractical. Foundations or sewer lines could not economically be dug through solid rock. So Roxaboxen continued—still there.

When the picture book *Roxaboxen* appeared, a note at the back gave the exact location of the hill. Yuma children read it and said to themselves: We know where that is! Although no soft earth was left, although the surface was now harsh, new lines of stone began appearing. Soon, Roxaboxen's neighbors began to see school buses visiting from other districts—making field trips to Roxaboxen.

Chapter IV of *The History of Roxaboxan* promised that Roxaboxen would rise again, and Marian's fifth chapter explained eloquently why it would do so. I'm looking forward to explaining how—but following her example, will leave the telling of those details for the final section!

The Fourth Avenue Grammar School (now a junior high school) stands only a few blocks from Roxaboxen. Marian's principal, Charles McGraw, still reigned there when Alice attended 6th-grade classes in 1944.

TWELVE

Roxaboxen
The Park

In the shadow of Black Hill on the southeast corner of Second Avenue and Eighth Street, in Yuma, Arizona there is a place known as ROXABOXEN . . .

The cover of a flyer for the Friends of Roxaboxen.

When the picture book *Roxaboxen* was published in 1991, many in the town of Yuma seemed as elated by its release as I. Thanks to Cecile (Cici) Marlowe, then the children's librarian at the Yuma County Library, and to Sandy Lobeck, chief librarian of Yuma School District One, I was brought to Yuma that fall to visit schools and celebrate the publication of the book.

Of course it was my mother, not I, who grew up in Yuma—but that fall I had the sensation of coming home.

A dream was born during that period. Those days were so busy for everyone, however, that it is now difficult to trace with clarity just how or when it emerged. Although it is possible the idea occurred to several people independently, I believe it was Marilyn Young—who, as I write, is now Mayor of Yuma—who first voiced it. She remembers that it was discussed with others just prior to my visit: Jerry Stuart, a Yuma businessman and member of the City Council; Nancy Cummings, Director for the Yuma County

Students in Mrs. Eager's class built miniature Roxaboxens. March 10, 1991. Corunna, MI.

Library District, and Bill Watkins, a retired Presbyterian minister. I myself first heard of it during a lunch I remember sharing with others — the table may have included Marilyn, Sandy, Cici, and Megan Reid, head of the Yuma Historical Society. Whatever the moment of birth, whoever the midwives, the idea was a simple one. Roxaboxen was still there. Why not try to protect and restore it? Children should be free to play there forever as Marian and her friends once had played. Protection and preservation might be simple if the City of Yuma could be interested in accepting the land as a city park. The main problem would be gaining title to the hill.

What we knew indicated that the land was essentially useless as a building site, a source of tax obligations rather than income. The same owner who had tried in vain to level Roxaboxen now lived in Phoenix. He was believed to be in financial difficulties. It seemed possible that he might be persuaded simply to donate the property to the City of Yuma— particularly if by doing so he might reap tax advantages. I volunteered to write him. On December 2, 1991, I sent to him and his wife a copy of the picture book, together with a letter that told them of Yuma's dreams and encouraged a generous gesture on their part. I indicated that if the land itself could be donated, we Doan descendants would be happy to pool our resources to cover the expenses of returning the hill to its original condition.

The response was a letter proposing that I or my family buy the land—at the price of $38,000, an amount that seemed to me breathtaking for a piece of land without real prospect of development. I learned that the owner also had approached the city of Yuma with the same proposal. The hill had, it seemed, suddenly become very valuable.

On January 27, 1992, in an e-mail message to my siblings and children, I reported his proposal and my response. I told them I had thought of quoting Mother at him (the bit in the last chapter about the mines of Roxaboxen offering more joy than cliffs of gold and silver) but had eventually settled for a more temperate letter.

> Dear Mr. B—[he had addressed me as "Alice"!],
>
> I had hoped that there might be tax advantages for you in the donation I suggested. (The land has, after all, not attracted any use in all these decades.) I'm sorry that you don't see that as the case.
>
> While we Doan descendants could have covered the modest costs of restoring the property to a "natural" state, a figure such as that you have set as purchase price is not within our means. I fear that the city of Yuma (I hear they have also been approached) is unlikely to be able to consider such a price either, especially in these hard economic times.
>
> I regret that the appearance of my book (and my sharing it with you) may have made it seem to you that the property might have acquired enhanced commercial value. I hope you will forgive me for having raised what I fear are false expectations.
>
> Perhaps it is better that Roxaboxen exist purely in memory and imagination.
>
> Sincerely,
> Alice McLerran

But while I assumed the matter must rest there, the undaunted citizens of Yuma began to organize. If the owner wanted money, they would try to raise it. A local appraiser volunteered to donate his services to appraise the property, and his appraisal set its value as $28,900. This figure struck many as still unrealistically high; it was not clear that the appraiser knew of the underlying rock that made development of the site

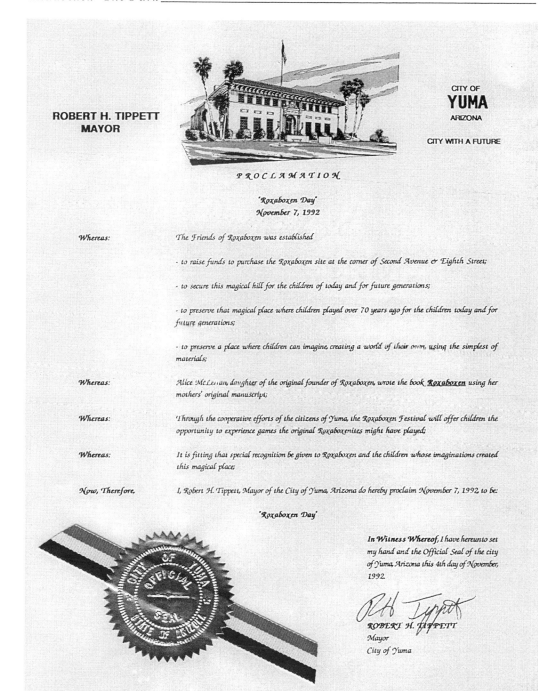

The Proclamation of Roxaboxen Day.

so difficult. The owner, however, certainly did! In any event, raising enough for a reasonable offer was a challenge the community was determined to meet.

Sandy Lobeck was the first chairperson of the "Friends of

The Mud Pie table at the fundraiser for the park.

Roxaboxen," a group that was established as a formal non-profit organization. The group quickly attracted civic leaders other than those already named. David Schuman, a local business-man, became active. One highly-motivated new member was Rosa Mielke, owner of a popular Yuma restaurant. She lived not far from the hill and knew how much the neighborhood children needed a place to play.

I loved hearing about the creative fund raising efforts going on in Yuma and was delighted to help share the brochure produced there with those everywhere who loved Roxaboxen. The "Friends of Roxaboxen" offered colorful titles to donors at different levels. Generous donors might have "deeds" to their own parts of the hill. I carried the brochure—and news of the Yuma effort—to schools and bookstores in a number of states. Teachers and librarians spread the word through their own grapevines. Donations soon began to come into Yuma from all over the country.

Soon, the "F r i e nds of Roxabox e n " offered Roxaboxen t-shirts and Roxaboxen hats. They searched out those

A close up of the creative mud pies.

places where the special pebbles that were Roxaboxen's money could be found. These were offered for sale too: individual pieces neatly boxed, with certificates of authenticity. This Roxaboxen money was especially popular with teachers and librarians who could pass around the treasure as artifacts whenever they read the story aloud.

Two Roxaboxen festivals, held in 1992 and 1993, raised impressive amounts of cash. Yuma schools participated—creating handicrafts to sell, running concessions and games. The City of Yuma offered its support, designating the day of the first festival as an official Roxaboxen Day.

Before the first festival took place, Cici—the children's librarian who had first helped bring me back to Yuma—moved to the midwest. Her successor at the Yuma County Library, Lisa Kniffin, became an outstanding asset to the "Friends of Roxaboxen." Her leadership of the festival committee helped make both celebrations lively ones, and she eventually became the second chairperson of the "Friends of Roxaboxen."

Those attending the festivals enjoyed games and contests that might have been played in 1915—egg toss, a three-legged race, musical chairs, a water-carrying relay and so forth. The vendors of Roxaboxen t-shirts wore period costumes, musicians both young and old played mariachi music, the mud pie contest elicited some spectacular entries. Rosa's culinary expertise let the "Friends" offer delicious Mexican food at reasonable prices to families attending. Everything that imagination could devise was offered to create a gala atmosphere on the broad lawns surrounding the Yuma County Library.

Kelsey and Whitney Kuptz, and their grandmother Marian Turner, stride forward for the Festival's 3-person ski race.

The festivals proved magnets for several generations of Doan family descendants. We joyously converged in Yuma not only with Marian's sisters Jean and Anna May, but with other original Roxaboxenites. Eleanor Winsor Davis drove up from Tucson with her husband; Estelle Dingus still lived in Yuma. Charles Miller was unable to leave his ailing wife to join us but was represented by his daughter—another Jean.

The family member who traveled farthest to be with us at the second festival was my cousin Carol, who flew down from Maine. Carol's daughter (named Robin after her aunt) had been ill for many years and was at that point very frail. But, she had been following Roxaboxen events with great interest, had in her hospital room a poster showing Barbara Cooney's luminous vision of Roxaboxen. Robin insisted her mother join the rest of us in Yuma. Carol flew into San Diego where she was met by her stepsister Ruth. As the two of them drove from San Diego to Yuma, rare rain clouds gathered over the desert. Carol remembers vividly that an "incredibly brilliant double rainbow" appeared as they crossed the dunes.

Carol called back to Maine, to the hospital or family there, frequently—with accounts of the joyous reunion to share with Robin. Learning that her daughter's condition was worsening, she returned a day early. Robin, unable to speak but mentally alert, was clearly delighted to be dressed in the Roxaboxen t-shirt her mother brought for her. She wore it for the remainder of her last day.

I like to think that Robin entered her final sleep as I had often fallen to sleep as a child—dreaming of that enchanted hill. Her mother likes to think that she awoke joyfully from that sleep to find that she could—like the Roxaboxen child silhouetted on her shirt—run freely once again.

However dear to generations of the Doan descendants the goal being pursued by the "Friends of Roxaboxen," however many others might share this vision as well, however energetic the fundraising, the fact remained that the organization's treasury still did not contain enough to tempt the owner to sell. He refused to budge from his original asking price. The "Friends" prudently used $5,066.59 of their funds to pay back taxes owed the county for the fiscal years 1986-92, giving them a lien on the property. They began to hope that the City of Yuma (to which an even larger amount in unpaid assessments was owed) could soon take the property to sell at auction, where "The Friends of Roxaboxen" could have a good chance of buying it. They might, indeed, be the only bidders!

The legal process that would allow the City of Yuma to take the land had already been initiated. Just before it could be completed, however, the hill's owner filed for protection under Chapter 11—using a chapter of the law that allowed him time to organize a plan to pay off his debts. A legal umbrella now protected his assets—and those assets included Roxaboxen. The City would have to wait.

The protection of the legal umbrella stayed in place—over long months that somehow turned to years.

While the City of Yuma and the official "Friends of Roxaboxen" remained frustrated by the owner's legal maneuvers, younger friends of Roxaboxen were quietly active. A contractor living in Phoenix might

Eleanor, Jean, and Alice signing books at the 1992 Roxaboxen Festival..

hold formal title to Roxaboxen, but the hill had acquired new caretakers. No matter who owned the land, play had resumed. Restoration was in fact already beginning. Neighborhood children were trying to clean and care for the hill as they staked out new houses there. Little by little, they gained access to the materials they needed. There were still plenty of rocks, of course! But as Barbara Cooney had observed when she visited Roxaboxen, the modern glass there consisted mainly of broken beer bottles from a nearby bar—pieces too sharp to use. Then, near the time of the 1993 Roxaboxen Festival, an anonymous donor left on Roxaboxen a luminous heap of real desert glass. It was eagerly seized upon and used by the young builders. The edges of this glass had been smoothed by windblown sand; the clear pieces had been turned to amethyst by desert sun. Once more, house could have jeweled windows.

At last in 1996, the "Friends of Roxaboxen" and the City of Yuma joined forces to make the owner an offer he couldn't refuse. The "Friends" provided $5,100 in cash to the deal to go to the owner and of course had already paid for back county taxes through 1992. The City contributed $3,910.66 for recording fees and for county taxes 1993-96, $2,097.50 for services of a bankruptcy lawyer, and forgave the $11,548.38 owed for unpaid street assessments. Yuma Title Company donated escrow costs.

The City of Yuma agreed to accept title to the land, to take responsibility for restoration of the hill, and to protect it as a natural desert park. A few small modifications would be necessary—allowing access by the handicapped, adding a plaque to identify the site as "Roxaboxen"—but in general the City simply would attempt to restore the contours and natural vegetation patterns of 1915. The dream that was born in 1991 is in the process of realization as I write.

I love to remember a moment back in 1993, when the "Friends of Roxaboxen" were hard at work raising funds, and I was describing their goal to a group of third-graders. When I mentioned the word "park," one girl raised her hand and asked in obvious alarm: "You mean they're going to put swings and stuff on Roxaboxen?"

Before I could respond, one of her classmates did. "No, silly—not like that. It's going to be a playground for the imagination."

Who could improve on such a definition?

Roxaboxen will always be there, inviting the imaginations of new builders. The "Friends of Roxaboxen" in Yuma, the friends of Roxaboxen everywhere, have helped fulfill the confident prophecies that ring in the last chapter of Marian's book. We need no longer fear that Roxaboxen must be deserted. Its citizens may forever cry, "Hurrah for Roxaboxen!"

Marian Doan

Helen Dunbar

Frances Doan

The CHILDREN